Secrets to Outlining a Novel

The Creative Story Outlining Method

Write Novels That Sell: Book 2

by K. Stanley and L. Cooke

Secrets to Outlining a Novel

Copyright © 2023 by K. Stanley and L. Cooke
All rights reserved.
Published by Fictionary Press
Library of Congress Cataloging-in-Publication
Data is in file with the publisher.
Trade Paperback ISBN: 978-1-9992762-8-7
e-Book ISBN: 978-1-999-2762-9-4
No part of this publication may be reproduced in any form, or by any means, electronic or mechanical, including photocopying, recording, or any information browsing, storage, or retrieval system, without permission in writing from the publisher.
Cover Design by K. Stanley and L. Cooke
Formatted in Affinity Publisher by K. Stanley and L. Cooke

Praise for Secrets to Outlining a Novel

"A fresh, actionable, step by clear step approach to creating a story outline that produces amazing results! Can't sing enough praises for Secrets to Outlining a Novel. Don't write your next novel without these insights, hints and tips."

Mary Buckham, USA bestselling author of Break Into Fiction: 11 Steps to Building a Powerful Story

"Writing a book is a huge (and scary) task. In Secrets to Outlining a Novel, Kristina and Lucy have demystified the process, breaking it down into approachable, bite-size pieces that help you understand outlining at both a macro and micro level."

Hayley Milliman, Head of Education, ProWritingAid

K. Stanley Dedication

To my mom.

For her encouragement to always be learning.

L. Cooke Dedication

To Mum and Dad.

Happy 50th Wedding Anniversary.

Chapter One: Introducing a Novel Outlining Process	9
Chapter Two: The End Goal	19
Chapter Three: Writing Your Skeleton Blurb	23
Chapter Four: Skeleton Synopsis Theory	41
Chapter Five: Let's Create the Skeleton Synopsis	47
Chapter Six: Outlining Act 1	69
Chapter Seven: Outlining the First Half of Act 2	95
Chapter Eight: Outlining the Second Half of Act 2	115
Chapter Nine: Outlining Act 3	133
Chapter Ten: The Full Story Outline	157
Chapter Eleven: Outlining a Scene	161
Chapter Twelve: Six Story Elements You Can't Live Without	173
Chapter Thirteen: Outlining the Five Story Arc Scenes	181
Chapter Fourteen: Bringing It All Together	217
Chapter Fifteen: Outlining Nonlinear Structures	225
Chapter Sixteen: Outlining Subplots	239
Chapter Seventeen: Where to Next After This Book?	243
Glossary	247
Index	255
Acknowledgments	265
About the Authors	269

Chapter One: Introducing a Novel Outlining Process

Let's Start Outlining

Everyone reading this book has a dream. You want to write a novel. Scratch that, you want to write a novel readers love.

Luckily, we know there is one universal factor for making readers love your story.

> **Readers love a story that is structurally sound.**

We know you have a super imagination, as you're a writer. The process we're about to share with you shows you how to get your story's structure sound before you write your draft.

This is the first secret we will unlock in this book.

How to outline a structurally sound story.

We'll share an actionable process and help you outline your story. Your story will be unique, spectacularly your own, AND structurally sound.

The process in this book will unleash your creative juices. You'll build an outline and create a framework for writing a well-loved story.

We believe writing a story makes your voice immortal. Stories must be strong enough to capture many readers, and this comes from building the structure into the story. You can work on story structure at any time during your writing process. However, the most efficient time is during the outlining phase.

Books landing on a bestseller list are stories readers love. The stories vary in a myriad of ways, and yet they all have one underlying aspect in common. They all have a structure the human brain can relate to. This structure has been around since Beowulf was first written, and it's still around today.

When we talk about outlining, we're talking about building a solid structure into your story. When you write the story, you'll spend your time focused on your artistry because you've already created the deep structure in your outline.

Congratulations

You've made the first step to making your book dreams come true. By being open to a new way of outlining you are:

- Being proactive.
- Open to outlining help.
- Doing what is necessary to create a novel readers love.

The great news is you have come to the right place.

Whether you're outlining romance, horror, fantasy, mystery, thriller, or any other genre, we have an actionable process you can use to create unique stories—repeatedly.

Our outlining process is not about creating a cookie cutter "samesy" story as all the other stories created. It is looking at a time-proven story structure and building your story outline from there.

Once you have the outline of your story laid out, your artistry, your voice, and your vision will make the story unique to you.

You may have heard the common advice, "Show, don't tell." When you show something to the reader, it takes more words than telling, and this means you need to be particular about what you include. Our outlining process gives you a method to only include what matters to the story. Only the good bits make it into the story, because only the good bits have a reason to be in the story.

We want your artistry to shine. We want your story to stand up and count. We want you to find your success.

Writing a Novel Is Huge

There is no way we can say writing a novel is anything but a mammoth task. And yet, a mammoth book writing task can be manageable and fun. The only way to finish a mammoth task is to have a comprehensive, objective, and actionable process.

In our book *Secrets to Editing Success: The Creative Story Editing Method*, we showed you how to edit a draft manuscript with a comprehensive, objective, and actionable process. We'll do the same here for outlining.

Outlining is not an all-or-nothing process. You can jump off the outlining train to get to your writing any time you like.

There are some significant benefits to just reading the first section of this book. There are even greater benefits to digging a little deeper into your outline to uncover more of the story structure. The greatest benefit comes from following the whole outlining process.

All of us create differently. All of us are individuals, and one of the many beauties of our outlining process is you can jump on and off as your muse grabs you.

Benefits of an Outlining Process

> **Our outlining process is about efficiency, a tight story line, and being organized.**

Our outlining process will spark your imagination and do away with the dreaded blank page.

Above all, our outlining process is creative.

This book gives you a step-by-step method to create your outlining masterpiece. For each step, we'll share how we outlined two of our novels. These are *Evolution* by K. Stanley and *My Fairy Assassin* by L. Cooke.

When you've finished outlining your story, you may want to keep going and outline your scenes. To get you started on scene outlining, we've added three bonus chapters later in this book. We'll show you how to outline a scene in depth. You can outline every scene in your novel using this process, so you create every scene based on a time-proven structure. You'll find this starting in Chapter Eleven: Outlining a Scene.

Just in case you want to delve into more complicated structures, we've added a fourth bonus chapter to show you how to outline complex structures, such as a dual narrative story. With the foundation we'll give you, you can create any story you dream of. You'll find this in Chapter Fifteen: Outlining Nonlinear Structures.

This book shows you how to outline the main plot line of your story. We've added a fifth bonus chapter to get you started on outlining subplots. You can find this in Chapter Sixteen: Outlining Subplots.

With all this knowledge at your fingertips, imagine how great your novel is going to be.

Where to Next?

We'll give you a quick overview of how to use this book. This book is about taking action and creating your outline as you read, so the next section is important. We'll follow that up with the end goal. We want to show you where you'll end up before you start outlining. This will give you a clear view of where you are in the process and why each step is important.

Right after that, you'll get started on the first step in outlining your novel. Without this first step, outlining is extremely difficult. With this step, it becomes easy.

How to Use This Book

Action rocks in fiction, and action rocks in outlining. In this book, you'll create your outline as you read. By the time you finish each chapter, you'll have another part of your outline created, and by the end of the book, you'll have your outline done. How's that for super productive?

By the time you've finished reading, you'll have an outline for your novel, and you can start writing. It won't just be an outline for any novel. It will be an outline for a novel with the potential to be a commercially successful book.

What Is Commercial Fiction?

Commercial fiction is where bestsellers live. They are books readers go to when they want a great story.

The very best of commercial fiction are novels with a strong story structure, crafted by authors in such a way that they appeal to many people.

They are the books readers love.

We're going to outline the events all stories need, no matter the genre. An engaging romance, fantasy, thriller, or young adult novel all have one thing in common. They are structured in a way that connects with the human brain.

> **In this book, we'll unlock the secrets of a well-structured story. After all, structure is the aspect that makes or breaks a book.**

Let's Meet the Outlining Process

Outlining is about taking a story promise and making sure the whole story keeps that promise. The story promise is why the reader picks up the story.

And the blurb on the back cover of a book contains the story promise. The story promise is the goal the protagonist is trying to achieve.

A skeleton blurb is a short version of the full blurb. The skeleton blurb is just for you, the author, and does not contain the ending of your story.

You'll start with a skeleton blurb and finish with an outline of the story structure with a beginning, middle, and end. This will include key scenes needed for the reader to connect emotionally with your story.

All processes, like all stories, start at the beginning.

Please don't skip the initial parts of the process, as they are the foundation of the entire process.

They are super simple, too. You can create the most powerful part of your outline in less than ten minutes. The speed does not come from a weakness. The speed comes from years of boiling down the essentials of story structure.

Outlining Step 1

Write your skeleton blurb.
This is your story promise. The promise must be strong; otherwise, your outline will not be strong.

Outlining Step 2

Create a Skeleton Synopsis.
A skeleton synopsis shows the beginning, middle, and end of your story. Outlining a skeleton synopsis is another easy step. You'll outline the five story arc scenes—the inciting incident, plot point 1, the middle plot point, plot point 2, and the climax, along with the resolution.

Outlining Step 3

Outline the Key Scenes in Act 1, Act 2, and Act 3.
Stories, no matter how different they are, how imaginative, how varied, all follow Aristotle's three act structure and contain a beginning, a middle, and an end. The fact is a book begins on page one and ends on the last page. We read linearly, even if the story's timeline is nonlinear.

With these beginnings, middles, and ends in mind, storytellers are happy to split their stories into sections when creating their story. These sections are called acts.

The first act is the beginning. The second act is the middle of the story action. And the third act is where the story ends. These act endings are not arbitrary. Act 1 ends with plot point 1, Act 2 ends with plot point 2, and Act 3 ends with the closing image.

We'll answer what goes into a beginning act, so your outline has all the ingredients of a great beginning.

We'll explain what goes into the middle act, and how to keep the story structure strong, taut, and on point.

Finally, we'll explore the end and learn how to make it fit the story. A satisfactory climax comes from one underlying structural factor: The protagonist either achieved the story goal or they didn't.

Get Ready to Work

You're going to outline along with us, and by the end of this book, you'll have written a structurally sound outline for your novel.

We'll share the theory together with actionable steps. We'll give you lots of freedom to make artistic decisions and choices. The actions will spur you to question your story, so it is stronger. Creating an outline will make the process of writing your first draft efficient.

After you've written a solid story outline, we'll give you a process to outline each scene. Chapter Eleven: Outlining a Scene, Chapter Twelve: Six Story Elements You Can't Live Without, and Chapter Thirteen: Outlining the Five Story Arc Scenes show you how to outline a structurally sound scene.

Chapter Fourteen: Bringing it All Together shows you how to choose the type of protagonist that fits your outline.

This book shows you how to outline a novel told in a linear way. In Chapter Fifteen: Outlining Nonlinear Structures, we've added a section on how to use your outline to create a nonlinear story.

We're going to focus on the main plot of your story. Without that, it's hard to create subplots. In Chapter Sixteen: Outlining Subplots, we'll show you how to add subplots to your outline.

What Is Outlining?

Outlining means you're listing the main events in your story instead of opening a blank page and writing without a plan.

The main event in every scene will take the protagonist closer to or farther away from achieving the main story goal. This is true even if the protagonist is not in a scene.

You can still be a pantser, often called a discovery writer, and create an outline. The outline gives you a starting point. When you go in directions you didn't expect, you can change the outline.

Once you've created an outline for your main plot, you'll have a process to use for more complicated structures. You can add subplots and scenes that build the character arc after you have a solid structure for your main plot.

You'll create the main outline as a list of scenes, but when you write the story, you may choose to combine some of the scenes into one scene. You may also choose to have more than one scene represent an event.

At this stage, we want to learn what the story is. The goal is to create an outline that you can change as you work on it.

Where to Next?

To get the most out of this book, create your outline as you read this book. By the time you reach the last page, you'll have an outline to follow while you write your first draft.

And we think that's amazing.

Let's take a look at the end goal before we start outlining.

Outlining   Secrets   Unlocked

Chapter Two: The End Goal

You'll create an outline for the key scenes in your novel.

We'll start with the skeleton blurb, followed by the skeleton synopsis. Then we'll outline the five story arc scenes. After that, we'll outline the scenes needed before and after the story arc scenes. Then, we'll outline Act 1, Act 2, and Act 3. From there, you'll go on and create other scenes that are unique to your novel.

We outline the five story arc scenes first because if one of these scenes is missing, there is no story. Let's do a quick review of why we need the five story arc scenes.

The inciting incident shakes up the protagonist's ordinary life.

> **If there is no inciting incident**
> **there is no story**
> **because all we're reading about is**
> **a protagonist's ordinary life.**

Plot point 1 shows the protagonist accepting the story goal.

> **If there is no plot point 1,**
>
> **meaning the protagonist doesn't accept the story goal,**
>
> **then there is no story**
>
> **because the protagonist doesn't do anything.**

The middle plot point shows the protagonist changing from reactive to proactive.

> **If there is no middle plot point,**
>
> **the protagonist doesn't drive the story forward and cause problems,**
>
> **and there is no story.**

Plot point 2 shows the protagonist at the lowest point in the story and gives the protagonist the final piece of information they need to address the story goal.

> **Without the new information learned in plot point 2,**
> **the protagonist cannot address the story goal.**
> **If they can never address the story goal,**
> **the story never ends.**
> **There is no story if there is no plot point 2.**

The climax scene shows whether the protagonist achieves the external story goal, or they don't.

> **If there is no climax scene where the protagonist addresses the story goal,**
> **there is no story**
> **because the story isn't over.**

The main purpose of the resolution is to give the reader closure after the climax scene. The reader will want to know what the protagonist's world looks like after they have addressed the story goal in the climax.

> **If there is no resolution,**
> **the story may have ended but the reader will not feel satisfied.**
> **You'll still have a story,**
> **only the reader might not read your next book.**

By starting your outline with the five story arc scenes and a resolution, you're guaranteed to create a strong story.

The five story arc scenes give you the spine of your story, and every other scene works to support that story.

Where to Next?

We'll start you off with the skeleton blurb. Please don't skip the next chapter. The skeleton blurb forms the basis of your outline.

Chapter Three: Writing Your Skeleton Blurb

The fastest way to outline a novel is to write a skeleton blurb first. Without a skeleton blurb, it's very difficult to know what your story is about.

By the end of this chapter, you'll have written your skeleton blurb. You can always refine your skeleton blurb later, so don't get stuck perfecting this.

What Is a Skeleton Blurb?

> **A skeleton blurb is one sentence that states the main plot of your story.**

A skeleton blurb contains the protagonist, the external story goal, and the story stakes. The blurb must answer three questions.

1. Who is the protagonist?
2. What is the external story goal?
3. What is at stake?

Name your Protagonist or Not

During the initial outlining phase, the protagonist doesn't need a name.

Are you surprised?

> **All you need to know at this stage is there is a protagonist.**

If you know the name, use the name throughout the process. If not, just use the word "Protagonist" to refer to that character.

The External Story Goal

The story goal is what the protagonist is trying to achieve.

> **By the end of the story, either the protagonist achieves the goal, or they don't; otherwise, there is no story.**

The story goal is critical to the success of your outline and the success of your novel. It is an external goal that drives the action in every scene.

The story goal must be specific, so you can measure each scene in your story against the story goal.

By measurable, we mean you must be able to determine whether each scene brings the protagonist closer to achieving the story goal or drives them farther away. This doesn't mean the protagonist must be in every scene. That's an artistic choice you'll make later.

The Story Stakes

The story stakes are what happens if the protagonist doesn't achieve the story goal. These story stakes must make the reader worry. After all, you write commercial fiction for the reader, don't you?

> **A worried reader keeps on reading to find out if the protagonist is successful or not.**

Skeleton Blurb Examples

We've included three skeleton blurbs below to show what we're striving for before we create a story outline.

The first skeleton blurb is for this book: *The Secrets to Outlining a Novel* by K. Stanley and L. Cooke.

The second book is *Evolution* by K. Stanley.

The third book is *My Fairy Assassin* by L. Cooke.

For *Secrets to Outlining a Novel* the Skeleton Blurb Is:

> **A successful writer who plans must create a structurally sound outline; otherwise, readers won't love the writer's story.**

We wrote our blurb for this book together. We wanted to include information on how to create an outline that gives the writer creative inspiration.

Our first question to answer was: Who is the protagonist?

It's a writer staring at a blank page, planning on being a success.

What is the writer trying to achieve?

Writing a story readers love.

The first step in writing a story readers love is writing a story outline that is set up to create a story readers love.

This led us to the skeleton blurb goal: Create a structurally sound outline.

And if this doesn't happen, what are the stakes?

The writer writes a book readers don't love. What a horrible thought. We all know how personal writing a novel is. And getting bad reviews is crushing. We don't want that to happen to anyone. So, the stakes are high.

The three parts of our skeleton blurb are:

> **Protagonist: A successful writer who plans**
> **Story Goal: Create a structurally sound outline.**
> **Story Stakes: Readers won't love the writer's story.**

In a full sentence, we have:

> A successful writer who plans must create a structurally sound outline; otherwise, readers won't love the writer's story.

For *Evolution* the Skeleton Blurb is:

> **Jaz Cooper must find out who killed her husband using her ability to see into a dog's mind; otherwise, she might die.**

The skeleton blurb came to me (K. Stanley) in the middle of the night.

My Yellow Labrador, Chica, was four years old. She had cancer, and we thought she was in her last few days. I wanted every moment I could get together. I crawled into bed with her in the spare room on the ground floor of our house. At the time, we lived in the mountains in bear country.

I curled around her, put my hand on her soft belly, and watched the movement push my hand up and down. Her breathing slowed, either into a deep sleep or maybe the moment we would lose her.

Chapter Three: Writing Your Skeleton Blurb

At the sound of an animal sauntering past the open window, Chica's hair stood on end, bristling against my skin. Her breathing quickened. A growl rose from deep in her throat.

She launched off the bed and lunged toward our dining room. I ran behind her.

A black bear looked in. Behind it, our fence was demolished.

Chica stood stiff-legged, back arched, and held her ground in front of me.

The bear was silent.

Chica showed her fangs, drool dripping from her lips, and growled.

I could feel her emotions and knew what she was thinking. This was a visceral moment and out popped the first vision of the skeleton blurb for *Evolution*.

> **A woman must use her ability to see into a dog's mind to solve a crime.**

With some creative thinking, I came up with the three parts of the skeleton blurb. I had to ask myself how I could make this personal. This is where I decided the crime was her husband being murdered. Then I needed some stakes. I decided that her life would be in danger if she didn't find out who killed her husband. So here we have the three parts of the skeleton blurb.

> **Protagonist: Jaz Cooper (I already know her name, so we'll use it throughout this book.)**
> **Story Goal: Find out who killed her husband using her ability to see into a dog's mind.**
> **Story Stakes: She might die.**

In a full sentence, we have:

Jaz Cooper must find out who killed her husband using her ability to see into a dog's mind; otherwise, she might die.

This is the level of detail you need to outline your story. You can add more details later. At this point, all I knew was the protagonist was a woman, she could see into a dog's mind, there was a crime, and she would solve the crime using this skill. I added the name Jaz Cooper later. For clarity, we've added her name from the start as we outline.

For *My Fairy Assassin* the Skeleton Blurb is:

> **Liv Wright must use the fairy time portal to save her fairy assassin sister; otherwise, a scientist will destroy the world.**

This skeleton blurb came to me (L. Cooke) when I was in the cherry orchard, angry gardening.

To deal with anger, one of the best remedies for me is to get outside and get my hands into the weeds. I was pulling out nettles, grasping each spikey plant, and loading them into a wheelbarrow.

And why was I angry gardening? I had read an online newspaper that morning.

I was angry with the state of the world. I was angry that greed trumped the environment, about world leaders who appeared to be bonkers. I was angry with the lack of transparency of what scientists were manufacturing in labs and about the future we are gifting our children.

What had we done to the world?

Gardening calms the worry, the fear, and the anger, almost as soon as I'm outdoors. Definitely, as soon as I get my hands mucky.

In the cherry orchard, we have lots of plants. In the herb borders, we have thyme, primulas (oxlips), and wild violets. In the hedges, we have honeysuckles (woodbine), musk roses, and Sweet Briar (Eglantine).

Unbeknownst to me, I had spent a lot of time gardening in the place Shakespeare describes in Midsummer Night's Dream.

> "I know a bank where the wild thyme blows, where oxlips and the nodding violet grows, quite over-canopied with luscious woodbine, with sweet musk-roses and with eglantine: there sleeps Titania sometime of the night, lull'd in these flowers with dances and delight."
>
> A Midsummer Night's Dream, Act 2 Scene 1

And whether it was the exertion of the gardening, or Titania had woken up and whispered this story into my head, I suddenly had the story blurb.

We could save the world with fairy magic. And a child had to sort out the mess adults had created.

Fortunately, we don't need to angry garden or have fairy magic to outline a story.

The three parts of the skeleton blurb are:

> **Protagonist: Liv Wright.**
> **Story Goal: Use the fairy time portal to save her fairy assassin sister.**
> **Story Stakes: A scientist will destroy the world.**

In a full sentence, we have:

> Liv Wright must use the fairy time portal to save her fairy assassin sister; otherwise, a scientist will destroy the world.

Where to Next?

It's time for you to write your skeleton blurb because you need this for every step in the outlining process. Whether you know who the protagonist is or not, that character needs a story goal.

The Story Goal

Why Start with the Story Goal?

The story goal gives the protagonist something to do. The movement through the story's pages comes from the protagonist chasing the story goal. Their movement is what we're going to outline first. By outlining the story goal first, the story's secrets open up to you.

A Strong Story Goal Is Addressable

A story goal is addressable when it's clear whether the protagonist can achieve the goal or not.

For *Evolution*, the goal is: Find out who killed her husband using her ability to see into a dog's mind.

Either the protagonist will find out who killed her husband, or she won't.

For *My Fairy Assassin*, the goal is: Use the fairy time portal to save her fairy assassin sister.

Either the protagonist will save her sister by time traveling, or she won't.

Both goals are addressable in a 'will they or won't they achieve the goal' way.

A Strong Story Goal Is External

A story goal is external, so by the end of the story, the reader knows if the protagonist was successful categorically or they failed disastrously. And bonus points if you make the ending bittersweet, meaning the protagonist was successful, but the success came at a cost.

The goals for *Evolution* and *My Fairy Assassin* are external. This means the protagonist must act to achieve the goal. They are not internal goals about fixing themselves. This is key to this stage of the outlining process.

With a measurable, external goal, the reader will know what to cheer for and know when the story is finished, as the goal will be achieved or not.

A Strong Story Goal Is Relatable

The reader spends a long time with the protagonist experiencing tension-filled turmoil, but if the reader can't relate to the story goal, they will put the book down. Why walk over hot coals, steal a car, or jump off a bridge into a torrent of water for a cup of coffee when there is another coffee shop on the other side of the street?

But if the coffee shop has a barista who is the love of the protagonist's life, and today the barista is finishing their last shift and marrying someone else, then perhaps the story goal of getting to the coffee shop on time is worthy of the plot.

Evolution: The goal is to find out who killed her husband using her ability to see into a dog's mind. Anyone who loves their husband can understand that drive, so the goal is relatable.

My Fairy Assassin: The goal is to time travel to save her sister. Family ties are universally understood, and we would do anything to save the life of someone we love. This is another relatable goal.

A Strong Story Goal Meets Genre Expectations

Readers resonate with a story goal. The mystery reader would not like to have a murder ignored, so solving a murder is absolutely the goal for this genre. A romance reader would be disappointed if the protagonist did not find their soul mate. A fantasy reader adores a story goal about magic.

Evolution is a mystery with a paranormal subplot, and the story goal is to find out who killed the protagonist's husband using her ability to see into a dog's mind. Both the mystery and paranormal aspects of the genre expectations are met.

My Fairy Assassin is a young adult (YA) fantasy novel, and the teenage protagonist's story goal is to use the fairy time portal to save her fairy assassin sister. The novel is clearly a fantasy because of the magical fairy aspect, and the teenage protagonist is the one who has the story goal. Again, genre expectations are met.

A Strong Story Goal Is Specific

If the goal is specific, outlining is easier, and the reader will quickly understand what the story is about. You can see we're thinking of the end goal: Getting that book published. By creating a strong story goal now, you're going to have a much easier time writing the full blurb for the back jacket of your novel. How exciting is that?

Your Fun Outlining Task

Write your story goal.

When you create the story goal, make sure it is:

- Addressable
- External
- Relatable
- In line with genre expectations
- Specific

Where to Next?

You need the story goal before you can create the story stakes, so please don't turn the page until you know what your story goal is.

After you create your story goal, we'll show you how to link the story goal to the story stakes.

High Stakes Are Reader Glue

If the stakes are high, the reader will follow the protagonist through the story.

If the stakes are high, you'll always be able to see trouble brewing, find places to add tension and conflict, and most importantly, have fun creating the outline.

So, What Do We Mean by High Stakes?

High stakes are stakes you and the reader care about. High stakes can be something at stake just for the protagonist, or they can be something at stake for the entire world.

Evolution: The stakes are at the individual level. Jaz will die.

My Fairy Assassin: The stakes are at the world level. The world ends.

Story Stakes Contain a Real or Metaphorical Death

Stakes are about the ending of something. An ending could be the end of a relationship, or it could be the ultimate ending, death.

> **To find your story stakes, ask yourself, "If the story goal is not achieved, what ends for the protagonist?"**

Stakes can be related to Maslow's hierarchy of needs. Maslow's hierarchy of needs starts at the basic need to stay alive from air, water, and food. The next levels of needs are the need for shelter, for relationships, and finally for a place in society.

The closer the stakes are to a drastic ending, the higher the stakes are, and the more the reader will follow the protagonist through the story.

When you can find a hint of death or an ending of sorts in your stakes, the reader will be glued to the story. The reader will believe the character will go to the extremes they do as the stakes motivate the protagonist.

Story Stakes Must Matter

The story stakes must matter to the reader. If the protagonist's story goal is to fix a spacecraft communications center; otherwise, they won't hear the latest intergalactic solar ball game results, the stakes won't matter.

Whereas if the spacecraft is hurtling toward an asteroid belt, the communication center is broken, and the spacecraft's captain must call for help but can't, the stakes matter.

Fixing the communication center is crucial in the second example. There are lives at stake.

Spend time on your story stakes, as these will make your story easier to outline. The tension and conflict in the story come from stakes. Tension and conflict keep the reader engaged. Tension and conflict keep you engaged as you outline your novel.

Evolution stakes:

> **. . . Jaz will die.**

This is great for the stakes. As we outline, it's critical to make the reader love Jaz, so they care whether she lives or dies.

My Fairy Assassin stakes:

> **. . . a scientist destroys the world.**

The end of the world is high stakes. The reader is worried about every character they meet in the book.

If the protagonist does not achieve her goal, the world ends. Life on Earth is over.

Story Stakes Must Be Specific

Did you notice the stakes for both books are specific? The reader will know why they are cheering for the protagonist to achieve their goal.

It is human nature to care about others. Reading creates empathy, and science backs this up. When reading, the same parts of the brain light up as if the reader were experiencing these events in real life. The reader experiences the fictional world, and so high stakes get their imaginations rocketing and their visceral reactions going. When reading, the reader experiences the story world as if it is real.

Your Fun Outlining Task

Write the stakes for your novel.

Make sure the stakes:

- Contain a real or metaphorical death.
- Matter.
- Are specific.

Where to Next?

Who is your protagonist? Who will chase the story goal you defined in the skeleton blurb? Let's find out.

The Protagonist

Let's look again at the skeleton blurb for this book.

> **A writer who plans must create a structurally sound outline; otherwise, readers won't love the writer's story.**

Starting an outline with an in-depth character description can lead to a situation where a writer has characters in search of a story. And when the writer cares more about the characters than the story, they may focus on the characters and not the story structure. This can lead to a story that is not structurally sound. Which means readers won't love the story no matter how lovable the characters are.

The following is our basis for what we're about to recommend.

> **The protagonist is the main character who tries to achieve the story goal. They are the character who has the most to lose if they fail to achieve the story goal.**

A story must have a protagonist. Sometimes the protagonist walks into your consciousness fully formed. Sometimes they are shy and reveal themselves slowly.

Don't worry.

Both ways to create a protagonist absolutely work.

Let's unlock another secret to outlining a novel:

You don't have to choose a protagonist yet.

You don't even have to know what type of protagonist you're going to write.

If your protagonist is clear to you, by all means add their name to the skeleton blurb.

If they're not clear, use the word "Protagonist" until you're ready. The important point is not to get stuck here. We're going to help you create an outline quickly, and we don't want you staying on any part of the process for too long.

It's easy to create characters who are looking for a story but don't have a story goal yet. Then you must spend time searching for the story that suits the character. It's more efficient to outline the story and add characters as you need them.

Types of Protagonists

We love to think of a protagonist as an entity. There are three types of protagonist entities.
1. A single protagonist: one main character on one adventure.
2. A combined protagonist: two main characters on the same adventure striving for the **same** story goal.
3. A group protagonist: many characters on different adventures striving for the **same** story goal.

Once you've created your story outline, you'll be able to see what type of protagonist entity suits your story.

If you want to show one character's struggles with the story goal, that is a single protagonist. Or if perhaps you want to show the duality of characters going after a story goal, a combined protagonist might be best. And if you want to show how a community must come together to achieve their story goal, then a group protagonist might be for you.

For now, imagine the combined or group protagonist as a single protagonist with a single goal. This will help you create a structurally sound outline. It will also help you decide what your protagonist strategy is after you've created your outline.

We really want you to focus on the outline, so we're not going to give you an in-depth description of the three entities yet. We're letting you know they exist, so you won't stress about the protagonist. We'll cover more on the different types of protagonist entities in Chapter Fourteen: Bringing it All Together.

Evolution

The first skeleton blurb for *Evolution* was: A woman must use her ability to see into a dog's mind to solve a crime. K. Stanley decided her name was Jaz Cooper very early on, so we'll use the name throughout this book.

My Fairy Assassin

The first skeleton blurb for *My Fairy Assassin* was: Liv Wright must use the fairy time portal to save her fairy assassin sister; otherwise, a scientist will destroy the world.

L. Cooke wanted a young adult to save the day. She wanted the protagonist to be a girl, as she had always seen the character as a female. This story is about living right, so you can see where the name came from.

Your Fun Outlining Task

1. Name your protagonist.

This is an easy one. Either refer to your protagonist as "Protagonist" as you outline or refer to them by a name. Remember, you can change or add a name at any time.

2. Write your skeleton blurb.

Since we're at the end of the chapter, you also have the task of writing your skeleton blurb in one sentence. You have everything you need to do this.

- The protagonist.
- The story goal.
- The story stakes.

The sentence looks like: <enter protagonist> **must** <enter story goal>; **otherwise**, <enter story stakes>.

As an example, let's review the skeleton blurb for *My Fairy Assassin*.

Liv Wright must **use the fairy time portal to save her fairy assassin sister**; otherwise, **a scientist will destroy the world.**

It's your turn now.

Where to Next?

The next step is where your story begins. And we don't mean page one. We're about to unlock the next secret of outlining your novel.

Chapter Four: Skeleton Synopsis Theory

If you've read *The Secrets to Editing Success: The Creative Story Editing Method* by us, K. Stanley and L. Cooke, you'll know about the skeleton synopsis.

In case you haven't read it yet, we're going to recap it here, because we need a skeleton synopsis to create a story outline. You'll find deeper information about a skeleton synopsis in Chapter Six of *The Secrets to Editing Success: The Creative Story Editing Method*.

The skeleton synopsis shows the deep structure of your story and gives you a way to prove the story promise is kept. The story promise is the story goal together with the story stakes.

You already know the story promise because you wrote it in your skeleton blurb.

The skeleton synopsis will guide you through creating a structurally sound outline. The outline will guide you through writing a structurally sound novel.

What Is a Skeleton Synopsis?

A story synopsis outlines the story in a summarized form.

It's usually written in present tense, shows the main plot line, and showcases the writer's voice.

> **A skeleton synopsis is the shortest form of a story synopsis.**

The skeleton synopsis does not highlight the writer's voice. It shows the outline of the story, including the skeleton blurb, the five story arc scenes, and the resolution.

The scenes included in the skeleton synopsis are:
- the inciting incident,
- plot point 1,
- the middle plot point,
- plot point 2,
- the climax
- and the resolution.

The purpose of a skeleton synopsis is to show you that you have the minimum number of scenes needed to keep the story promise and to create a structurally sound story. A skeleton synopsis is for you to use while you're outlining, writing, and editing your novel, and it forms the basis of a story synopsis.

The Skeleton Synopsis Structure

This is the structure of a skeleton synopsis.

> **Skeleton Synopsis = Skeleton Blurb + 5 Story Arc Scenes + Resolution**

We'll use part of the skeleton synopsis to create the first version of your story outline. The skeleton blurb and the five story arc scenes are all we need to get started.

The resolution details will come when we outline Act 3.

For now, all you need to know is whether your story ends with the protagonist achieving their story goal or not. Once you know that, you can carry on to the most powerful part of the outlining process.

In *Evolution*, Jaz will find out who murdered her husband.

In *My Fairy Assassin*, Liv will save her sister and the world.

Everything we outline will lead to the outcome we want.

We're going to outline the five story arc scenes first.

Why?

Because these scenes are fulfilling the deepest part of the story promise (the story goal and stakes). All scenes need to be related to the story goal, but in the five story arc scenes, the protagonist interacts with the story goal in a specific way.

What Is Scene Mirroring?

Imagine standing in front of a mirror. The reflection does all the opposite actions to what you are doing. We use a similar concept with scenes.

Mirroring is a scene that has opposite actions to the ones in a mirroring position.

If at the start of the story everyone is happy, then the mirror to that story could be that it ends in a tragedy. If a story starts with a single person, then the mirror could be they end up in a relationship.

In the context of the five story arc scenes, plot point 1 mirrors plot point 2. If in plot point one, the protagonist is naïve with regards to the story goal and then in plot point 2, due to new information, either internal or external, they gain an understanding, then we have scene mirroring.

The image below shows which scenes mirror each other.

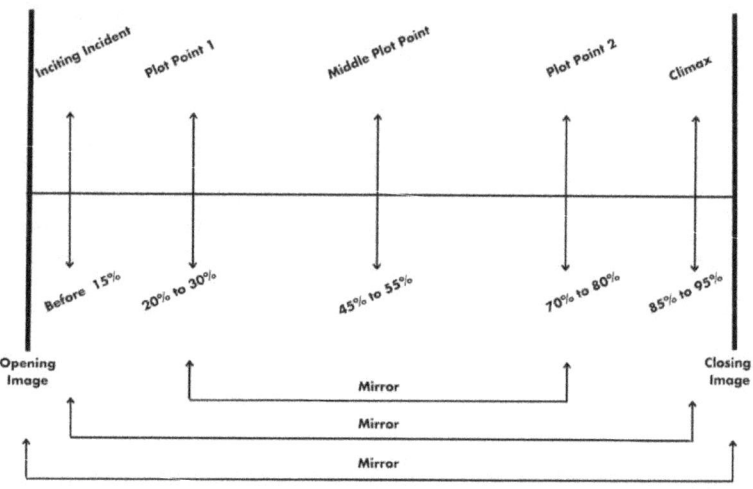

Outlining the Story Arc Scenes First

We've created a process to help you avoid writer's block and to make sure your story is structurally sound. The skeleton synopsis will help.

You've already written the first part of the skeleton synopsis, and that's the skeleton blurb. We recommend you outline the five story arc scenes next.

- Inciting Incident
- Plot Point 1
- Middle Plot Point
- Plot Point 2
- Climax

We recommend this because if one of the story arc scenes is missing, there is no story.

Refer to your skeleton blurb. There are hints in the skeleton blurb that will lead you to the main events in the five story arc scenes. When we first realized this, it was an outstanding discovery. One that made our skin sizzle. You know the moment when you finally understand something? This was a moment for us.

Are you ready for it?

Shhhh. Don't tell anyone. We're about to unlock another creative story outlining secret...

The secret is you don't outline your novel in sequential order, just like you didn't outline your skeleton blurb in sequential order. You outline the scenes by building on the skeleton blurb and creating the skeleton synopsis in a nonlinear way.

We're going to show you one possible order to outline your scenes.

If you get an idea for a different order, outline what comes naturally to you.

The first scene we outline is plot point 1. It's not the opening image, it's not the inciting incident. It's plot point 1.

Why?

Because plot point 1 is where your protagonist decides to go after the story goal. It is the true start of the story.

Your Fun Outlining Task

Here you get off easy. This chapter was all about theory. Come back and reference it as you outline your novel.

Where to Next?

The next part of your outlining journey is to create the main events for the five story arc scenes.

This is going to be such fun, as you'll see how the skeleton blurb unlocks the outlining process.

Chapter Five: Let's Create the Skeleton Synopsis

Creating the Main Events

When creating an outline, everything builds from the skeleton blurb. Our goal for you is by the end of this book, you'll have created a structurally sound outline that you'll use to write your first draft.

The outline is a guide and is not set in stone. Some or all of the outline may change, and we recommend you keep moving forward with your outline even if you don't have all the answers.

We're going to outline a novel in an order that promotes speed and sparks creativity.

Let's unlock the next secret to outlining a novel.

If you create the outline of the five story arc scenes, but not in the order those scenes occur in the story, the ideas for each scene will come fast and furiously.

To create the outline, you'll generate a one-line statement showing the main action in each of the five story arc scenes.

We call this statement the main event for the scene.

This gives you the first level of detail for your outline.

Scene Main Event

At this stage in the outlining, a scene main event is the primary action in a scene written in a sentence or two. You can start out with general main events, so you don't get stuck. When you're ready, you'll make them more specific.

Once you list the main event for the five story arc scenes, the story will have focus. These main events will lead you through outlining your novel.

The synopsis outline you create will highlight structural issues before you've written a word of your story. You're building the skeleton synopsis to help you write a story where you control the readers' emotions. When you're an expert at structure, you're an expert at controlling readers' emotions. When you're an expert at controlling readers' emotions, you'll create a page-turning novel.

We're guessing you really want to know the order of creating the outline. The secret we've been so eager to unlock for you.

Chapter Five: Let's Create The Skeleton Synopsis

The Scene Outlining Order
Main event in plot point 1
Main event in the inciting incident
Main event in plot point 2
Main event in the climax
Main event in the middle plot point

We can hear your concern.

We're all following the same process, so how will our books be unique?

A process is about unlocking your individuality. You make each book unique because you are unique. For example, your idea for plot point 1 will differ from our idea. That's where artistry comes into play. Even if we all come up with the same skeleton blurb, we will all write unique books.

Our method helps you figure out the three acts of the story. Act 2 takes up fifty percent of the story and is often the hardest to write. By using the order we listed above, you'll be framing Act 2 with an outline for Act 1 and Act 3. That makes Act 2 easier to outline.

Did you notice something super cool about the order above?

By outlining plot point 1 first, it makes it easy to find the main event in plot point 2 because in a strong story, plot point 1 and plot point 2 mirror each other. This will show you what's needed in plot point 2.

The inciting incident and the climax also mirror each other. By outlining the inciting incident first, it makes it easy to find the main event in the climax. The main event in the climax must also show if the protagonist achieved the story goal or not. So, you see, we already have assets we can use to find out what's in our scenes.

1. Main Event in Plot Point 1

The main event in plot point 1 is the moment the protagonist reactively decides to chase the story goal.

Plot point 1 happens somewhere between twenty and thirty percent into the story. We're listing the placement of the scenes, so as you outline and then draft your story, the placement guides you to a strong structure.

The protagonist's decision is a reaction to an event that forces them to strive for the story goal. All other choices have been taken away from them. If they don't have to go after the story goal, they won't, and there is no story. This means the event must motivate the protagonist to accept the story goal written in your skeleton blurb.

Plot point 1 must:
1. Be told from the protagonist's point of view.
2. Be written in active form.
3. Cause the protagonist to reactively accept the story goal.
4. Mirror plot point 2.

2. Main Event in the Inciting Incident

The main event in the inciting incident hints at the story goal written in your skeleton blurb. The event is not strong enough yet to motivate the protagonist to accept the story goal. The protagonist might not know what the story goal is yet, but you do.

The inciting incident happens before fifteen percent into the story.

The main event in the inciting incident is the start of the threat you've stated as the stakes in the skeleton blurb.

The reader and the protagonist meet the story goal at the same time. Every scene before this scene is about setting up the ordinary world. We'll get to those scenes later.

Knowing the main event in plot point 1 makes creating the main event in the inciting incident easier because it must lead to the plot point 1 main event.

The inciting incident must:
1. Be told from the protagonist's point of view.
2. Be written in active form.
3. Cause the protagonist to react to the action. The reaction is the start of the protagonist's journey.
4. Be related to the story goal stated in the blurb.
5. Mirror the climax scene.

3. Main Event in Plot Point 2

The main event in the plot point 2 scene causes the protagonist to be at their lowest point in the story. Disaster has struck, and they believe they won't achieve their story goal. The reader will worry too.

Plot point 2 happens somewhere between seventy and eighty percent into the story.

All hope and all other options must be lost in this scene. Here the protagonist learns the final piece of information they need to address the story goal.

Plot point 2 is a special plot point because it has two parts. The first half of plot point 2 is the lowest point in the story for the protagonist. The second half of plot point 2 is when the protagonist picks themselves up and goes after the story goal no matter the consequences.

For our outlining process, we're putting the first half of plot point 2 in one scene. The second half of plot point 2 will come in the scene called Reaction to Plot Point 2. We'll cover the reaction scene later when we outline Act 3.

Plot point 2 must create a sense of urgency. You want the reader to feel the urgency, so they don't stop reading.

This scene will mirror plot point 1, and we already know the main event in plot point 1, so this triggers ideas for plot point 2.

Plot point 2 must:
1. Be told from the protagonist's point of view.
2. Be written in active form.
3. Cause the protagonist to be at their lowest emotional point of the story so far.
4. Share the final piece of information the protagonist needs to address the story goal.
5. Create a sense of urgency.
6. Mirror plot point 1.

4. Main Event in the Climax

The main event in the climax occurs when the protagonist either achieves the story goal as stated in the skeleton blurb or they don't. You can understand why we said the story goal must be addressable, external, and specific. You'll need to show the protagonist in action, fighting for the story goal.

The climax happens somewhere between eighty and ninety percent into the story.

This can be a positive moment, which is a happy-ever-after moment. It can be a negative moment, and the protagonist fails. Or it can be bittersweet where the protagonist is successful but at a great cost.

The climax scene must:
1. Be told from the protagonist's point of view.
2. Be written in active form.
3. Show the protagonist leading the action.
4. Show the protagonist addressing the story goal.
5. Mirror the inciting incident.

5. Main Event in the Middle Plot Point

The middle plot point is the connecting scene between the first and second half of Act 2.

The main event in the middle plot point causes the protagonist to change from being reactive to proactive with regards to the story goal.

The middle plot point happens somewhere between forty-five and fifty-five percent into the story.

The protagonist realizes the value of the story goal and now takes action to drive the story forward.

Once you know the main event in the middle plot point, outlining Act 1, Act 2, and Act 3 becomes easier. All scenes before the middle plot point must lead to the main event in the middle plot point.

Every main event after the middle plot point is a result of the main event in the middle plot point.

You can use the main event in the middle plot point as your lighthouse.

The middle plot point must:
1. Be told from the protagonist's point of view.
2. Be written in active form.
3. Show the protagonist leading the action by the end of the scene.
4. Show the protagonist proactively wanting to address the story goal.
5. Foreshadow the ending.

Does this Process Have to be in this Order?

That's up to your imagination.

The above is the most efficient order to create a working skeleton synopsis. We designed the process in this order because as you proceed through the scenes, you'll build on the previous scenes.

It is not the only way.

The process is about finding each of the scenes.

If you sit down with your skeleton blurb and you have a sudden inspiration for the main event in the climax, go for it. Write it down.

If you know what the lowest moment in the book looks like. Then you have plot point 2. Write it down.

The key to this method is to outline the five story arc scenes. The order the muses speak to you might vary.

> **Creating the main events for the five story arc scenes is the key to a structurally sound outline.**

Your Fun Outlining Task

Review your skeleton blurb, and remind yourself of who the protagonist is, what their story goal is, and what's at stake if they don't achieve the story goal.

Next write out this list in this order.
1. Skeleton blurb
2. Plot point 1
3. Inciting incident
4. Plot point 2
5. Climax
6. Middle plot point

This is not the order the scenes will be in your first draft. It's the order that will make it easy for you to outline your novel. Don't worry about the resolution yet. We'll get to that later in this book.

Where to Next?

In the next two sections, we'll show you how we outlined the five story arc scenes for *Evolution* and *My Fairy Assassin*. You'll create the main event of your five story arc scenes right along with us. Outlining the five story arc scenes is critical to creating a structurally strong outline, so please don't skip it. By the end of this chapter, you'll know your main plot.

Chapter Five: Let's Create The Skeleton Synopsis

Outlining the Story Arc Scenes

Evolution Story Arc Scenes

Outlining Plot Point 1

To outline plot point 1, we need to use the all-important skeleton blurb. We're going to make a bold statement. Without a skeleton blurb, it's impossible to outline plot point 1 AND ensure the story structure will be strong.

The main event in plot point 1 is where the protagonist accepts the story goal stated in the skeleton blurb.

To help you through the process, we'll show you what we mean using *Evolution* and *My Fairy Assassin* as examples. We'll show how we determined the main events in the plot point scenes.

In *Evolution*, the skeleton blurb is:

> **Jaz Cooper must find out who killed her husband using her ability to see into a dog's mind; otherwise, she might die.**

The first decision the skeleton blurb triggered was: Does Jaz's husband get murdered on the page, or is he dead before the story starts?

We decided Jaz's husband was dead before the story starts. This means the obvious action in plot point 1 is Jaz discovers her husband was murdered. Her goal in the skeleton blurb is to find out who murdered her husband, so in plot point 1, she must find out that he was murdered.

We also know she discovers this by seeing into a dog's mind or the scene won't relate to the skeleton blurb. We don't know what the action is yet, but we have a framework.

We decided the main event in plot point 1 for *Evolution* is:

> **Jaz uses a dog vision and finally believes her husband was murdered.**

Outlining the Inciting Incident

With plot point 1 defined, we move on to the inciting incident. We need to find an action that could cause the action in plot point 1 to happen. Can you see how easy this becomes as we connect the story using the story arc scenes?

Without an inciting incident, the protagonist's life goes on as usual and there is no story. The inciting incident must be connected to the skeleton blurb and to plot point 1.

For *Evolution*, Jaz's husband is already dead, so the only part of the skeleton blurb that applies to the inciting incident is Jaz's ability to see into a dog's mind. Jaz doesn't find out her husband didn't die in an accident until plot point 1, so we can't use the murder at this point.

Let's dive deeper into what the inciting incident must do. It's the moment the protagonist's world changes in a dramatic way. We'd say gaining the ability to see into a dog's mind is a dramatic change.

We decided the main event in the **inciting incident** is:

> **Jaz saves a dog's life and gains the ability to see into the dog's mind.**

This works because linking the ability to see into a dog's mind leads to the method she uses to discover her husband was murdered in plot point 1.

Chapter Five: Let's Create The Skeleton Synopsis

Outlining Plot Point 2

Plot point 2 is the lowest moment for the protagonist. Usually, their actions from the middle plot point forward have caused the disaster that will happen in plot point 2. You can get ideas for plot point 2 from the skeleton blurb, the inciting incident, or plot point 1. The main event in plot point 2 will mirror the main event in plot point 1.

At this stage, the action can be vague. We don't know who the supporting characters are yet. Everything we're doing is going to help us figure out the middle plot point. By knowing what disaster happens in plot point 2, we'll be able to figure out what we need in the middle plot point.

So far, we know:

Inciting Incident:

Jaz saves a dog's life and gains the ability to see into the dog's mind.

Plot Point 1:

Jaz uses a dog vision and finally believes her husband was murdered.

If we want plot point 2 to mirror plot point 1, and we do, then death seems like a good action that would mirror plot point 1 and bring Jaz to her lowest point. We also know to stay true to the skeleton blurb. Jaz must use the dog's visions to get her from the middle plot point to plot point 2.

We decided the main event in plot point 2 is:

Jaz's actions cause someone close to her to die.

This means Jaz is at her lowest point as she loses someone close to her because of her actions. The skeleton blurb shows us Jaz is trying to figure out who murdered her husband. Chasing this goal puts her life in danger, but she loses someone else instead. It all comes back to the skeleton blurb.

Outlining the Climax

The climax must relate to the skeleton blurb. In fact, the main event in this scene must show if the protagonist achieves the story goal stated in the skeleton blurb.

This one is easy to outline. We decided Jaz will succeed in achieving the story goal.

For *Evolution*, in the climax we want Jaz to use a dog's vision to discover who killed her husband.

You'll have noticed we brought in dog visions, so we stay true to the skeleton blurb.

So now we have:

Inciting Incident:

Jaz saves a dog's life and gains the ability to see into the dog's mind.

Plot Point 1:

Jaz uses a dog vision and finally believes her husband was murdered.

Plot Point 2:

Jaz's action causes someone close to her to die.

We decided the main event in the **climax** is:

> **Using a dog's vision, Jaz discovers who killed her husband.**

Jaz saves a life in the inciting incident and finds out who took a life in the climax. We like how these scenes mirror each other.

Outlining the Middle Plot Point

We're now at the middle plot point. Here, the protagonist moves from reactive to proactive behavior. This plot point must be the start of the protagonist going down the wrong or difficult path.

In *Evolution*, Jaz should learn something new about the antagonist and decide she's going after them. This must involve her skill of seeing into a dog's mind, or it won't relate to the blurb.

We decided the main event in the **middle plot point** is:

> **Jaz sees a new dog vision. She misinterprets the vision, and it leads her on the wrong path to finding her husband's killer.**

Here is what we have so far for *Evolution*:
We've made the key words bold to make sure each of the main events for the story arc scene relates to the skeleton blurb.

Skeleton Blurb:
Jaz Cooper must find out who **killed her husband** using her ability to **see into a dog's mind;** otherwise, she might **die.**

Inciting Incident:
Jaz saves a dog's life and gains the ability to see into **the dog's mind.**

Plot Point 1:
Jaz uses a **dog vision** and discovers her husband was **murdered.**

Middle Plot Point:
Jaz sees a new **dog vision.** She misinterprets the vision, and it leads her on the wrong path to **finding her husband's killer.**

Plot Point 2:
Jaz's action causes someone close to her to **die.**

Climax:

Using **a dog's vision**, Jaz discovers who **murdered her husband.**

Already our outline is giving us ideas on how to write the story. You can see this gives ideas for a resolution. For *Evolution*, Jaz figures out who killed her husband. This gives her closure. But she's lost a friend and must figure out how she's going to live with the consequences.

Now that we have the main events, we'll name the scenes as follows:

INCITING INCIDENT: Jaz can see into a dog's mind.

PLOT POINT 1: Jaz learns husband murdered.

MIDDLE PLOT POINT: Jaz misinterprets dog vision.

PLOT POINT 2: Jaz causes someone to die.

CLIMAX: Jaz finds murderer

We put the scene purpose in capital letters, so it's easy to see as we add more scenes.

Where to Next?

Let's see the whole process again with *My Fairy Assassin*. Once you see the creativity outlining sparks, you'll see how it can influence your story.

My Fairy Assassin Story Arc Scenes

Outlining Plot Point 1

The skeleton blurb for *My Fairy Assassin* is:

> **Liv Wright must use the fairy time portal to save her fairy assassin sister; otherwise, a scientist will destroy the world.**

In *My Fairy Assassin*, the stakes are high. The world will be destroyed if Liv doesn't save her sister. We thought Liv needed a personal reason to time travel. Something she couldn't back out of. So, we decided Liv's sister was dying, and if Liv didn't time travel, she couldn't save her sister.

We decided the main event in **plot point 1** is:

> **Liv's sister is dying, and Liv must learn to time travel to save her.**

Outlining the Inciting Incident

With plot point 1 defined, we move on to the inciting incident. We need to find an action that could cause the main event in plot point 1 to happen.

Without an inciting incident, the protagonist's life goes on as usual and there is no story. The inciting incident must be connected to the skeleton blurb and to plot point 1.

For *My Fairy Assassin*, we know in plot point 1, Liv's sister is dying, and Liv must time travel to save her. Before plot point 1 happens, Liv must learn that her sister's life is in danger but not understand she can do something about it.

Based on this, we decided the main event in the **inciting incident** is:

> **Liv discovers her sister is not dead yet but is stuck in a dying fairy world.**

We hope you noticed what we did there. By defining the action in plot point 1, referring to the skeleton blurb, and by recalling what an inciting incident must do, we came up with the main event in the inciting incident for *My Fairy Assassin*. This is exactly what we did for *Evolution*, and you can do it for your story, too.

Outlining Plot Point 2

Plot point 2 is the lowest moment for the protagonist. Usually, their actions from the middle plot point forward cause the disaster that will happen in plot point 2. You can get ideas for plot point 2 from the skeleton blurb, the inciting incident, and plot point 1.

At this stage, the action can be vague. We don't know who the supporting characters are yet. Everything we're doing is going to help us figure out the middle plot point. By knowing what disaster happens in plot point 2, we'll be able to figure out what we need in the middle plot point.

Plot point 2 is a mirror of plot point 1.

So far, we know:

Inciting Incident:

Liv discovers her sister is not dead yet but stuck in a dying fairy world.

Plot Point 1:

Liv's sister is dying, and Liv must learn to time travel to save her.

At this point, we don't know how Liv time travels. It doesn't really matter. We're going to assume she uses a time portal. That's all we need to know. By plot point 2, she is in a different time and needs to get back. Since we want plot point 2 to mirror plot point 1, it seems reasonable Liv must time travel again. Only this time, there's a problem.

We decided the main event in **plot point 2** is:

> **The time portal fails, and Liv cannot save her sister.**

Outlining the Climax

In the climax, the protagonist must do something to either achieve or fail to achieve the story goal set out in the skeleton blurb.

This one is easy to outline. We decided Liv will achieve the story goal. We also know the skeleton blurb for *My Fairy Assassin* is:

> Liv Wright must use the fairy time portal to save her fairy assassin sister; otherwise, a scientist will destroy the world.

This tells us the scientist must be in the climax scene. We decided the main event in the **climax** is:

> **Liv saves her sister by reopening the time portal and injuring the scientist.**

So now we have:

Inciting Incident:

Liv discovers her sister is not dead yet but stuck in a dying fairy world.

Plot Point 1:

Liv's sister is dying, and Liv must time travel to save her.

Plot Point 2:

The time portal fails, and Liv cannot save her sister.

Climax:

Liv saves her sister by reopening the time portal and injuring the scientist.

Now all we have left is the middle plot point.

Outlining the Middle Plot Point

In the middle plot point, the protagonist moves from reactive to proactive. This plot point must be the start of the protagonist going down the wrong or difficult path.

We know when Liv accepts the story goal in plot point 1, she accepts she must time travel. It makes sense the first time travel happens in the middle plot point. We don't know what the wrong path is yet, and that's okay. We can create that when we outline second half of Act 2.

We decided the main event in the **middle plot point** is:

Liv time travels to save sister.

Here is what we have so far for *My Fairy Assassin*:

We've put in bold the key words to show how each plot point relates to the skeleton blurb.

Skeleton Blurb:

Liv Wright must use the fairy **time portal** to save her fairy assassin **sister**; otherwise, a scientist will destroy the world.

Chapter Five: Let's Create The Skeleton Synopsis

Inciting Incident:

Liv discovers her **sister** is not dead yet but is stuck in a dying fairy world.

Plot Point 1:

Liv's **sister** is dying, and Liv must learn to **time travel** to save her.

Middle Plot Point:

Liv **time travels** to save **sister**.

Plot Point 2:

The **time portal** fails, and Liv cannot save her **sister**.

Climax:

Liv saves her **sister** by reopening the **time portal** and injuring the scientist.

In *My Fairy Assassin*, Liv will do anything to save her sister, but her actions will have consequences. We've built conflict deep into the story structure.

Now that we have the main events, we'll name the scenes as follows:

INCITING INCIDENT: Liv's sister stuck in time portal.

PLOT POINT 1: Liv's sister is dying.

MIDDLE PLOT POINT: Liv time travels to save sister.

PLOT POINT 2: Time portal fails, and Liv cannot save her sister.

CLIMAX: Liv saves sister.

We put the scene purpose in capital letters, so it's easy to see as we add more scenes.

Your Fun Outlining Task

Here's how you put it together.

Create the main event for each of the five story arc scenes in the following order just as we did for *Evolution* and *My Fairy Assassin*.
1. Plot point 1
2. Inciting incident
3. Plot point 2
4. Climax
5. Middle plot point

Along with the main event, name each scene and include its purpose in capital letters. You can now put the scenes in sequential order and include the main event.

If you've read *Secrets to Editing Success: The Creative Story Editing Method*, you'll know we recommended naming each scene in three words or fewer. This restriction is unnecessary at the outlining stage. We don't expect the scenes to have this level of focus yet. You can name each scene in three words or fewer after you've written the draft and are ready to edit.

For now, name the scenes using the words you need to get the idea across. The outline is your first pass at getting the story told.

Where to Next?

You may be so excited you'll be tempted to start writing. That's great but try not to do this.

The structure you already have will keep you on track, but if you keep outlining, the structure will be stronger. If you keep outlining, you may revise what you've outlined so far, and knowing that before you write any scenes will save a ton of time.

So, stay with us. Your creativity will fly with speed when you use a bit more structure.

We have a high-level outline of the story. This is the start of a skeleton synopsis. Next, we're going to discover what happens in Act 1.

Chapter Six: Outlining Act 1

Act 1 is the first quarter of the story you're outlining. And when you're outlining, you'll find deeper structural success when you know the purpose of each scene placement within each act.

Act 1 is the story setup. Act 2 kicks off the story, increases conflict, and shows the story's theme. Act 3 shows the consequences of everything that happened in Act 2.

The reader has high expectations of Act 1.

Act 1 must:
1. Draw the reader into the novel.
2. Introduce the reader to the story world.
3. Introduce the reader to characters.
4. Introduce the reader to the plot.
5. Set up and propel the reader through the rest of the book.

Since you've only outlined the five story arc scenes, you don't know the details behind the outline. We hope you have the skeleton of your story clear in your mind. You may have ideas for characters. You may have ideas for backstory. We're sure you have lots buzzing around about your story world.

As you outline the three acts, try not to add too much detail yet. We want you to have a strong story outlined before you spend time writing your scenes. We're building a framework for you to use when you write your draft.

One more guiding principle:

> **The main event for each scene shows what the event is and not how the event happens. Focusing on the "what" will help you avoid filling in too many details.**

For example, in *My Fairy Assassin*, the main event for the middle plot point is Liv time travels. We don't know how she does that yet.

The outline you create is to clarify the story in your mind. No one else needs to see it.

As we create the outline, we're going to give you a list of scenes to add for each act. If ideas for other scenes spring into your imagination, add those scenes to your outline and keep going. You can move or change them later.

Outlining Delivers the Act 1 Requirements

When you read a book, think about how you like to experience reading new information. Readers are just like you. If there is too much information at once, the reader can feel overwhelmed and get lost. Outlining will keep you from over-sharing too much too quickly. Instead, you'll craft each new gem of information, so the reader feels they are on a treasure hunt, enjoying the journey from one gem to the next, rather than beneath an info dump truck that is unloading its contents.

Outlining is a cure for the info dump curse. Just in case you haven't heard the term, an info dump occurs when large portions of backstory or setting are shared in a scene. It becomes an info dump when the information doesn't move the present story forward and is not incorporated into the action of the present scene. If the information answers all the questions a reader has, why would they read on? It is better to consider adding a small gem that the reader can piece together.

Act 1 is the place where a reader, or an agent, or a buyer, or a critic decides this is a story they want to invest in.

When you outline, you know your deep structure is strong enough to get these important readers to read your book. The first act will be strong enough to become a bestseller. We're not saying you can't get a bestseller without outlining. We just believe you can get there faster with an outline.

Let's Begin Act 1

We're going to add five new scenes to the outline in Act 1. These five scenes are:
1. Opening image
2. Lead-up to the inciting incident
3. Reaction to inciting incident
4. Resistance to story goal
5. Lead-up to plot point 1

The inciting incident can happen in the first scene. When this happens, the opening will be a quick view of the ordinary world.

The opening image and the lead-up to the inciting incident can be in the same scene as the inciting incident. This means one scene must work hard to fill the shoes of three scenes.

For the sake of clarity, to outline, we'll list the main events in these scenes as separate scenes. This is an outline for us to use as a structure to write the story. You'll organize the scenes during the drafting phase.

Before we get to outlining, let's review what each scene must do.

Opening Image

The opening image hooks the reader. Before the inciting incident happens, the story must show the protagonist's ordinary world. Then the reader knows what is at stake for the protagonist, and this adds tension to Act 1.

Lead-Up to the Inciting Incident

The scene right before the inciting incident is the last time the protagonist will experience their ordinary world. As the inciting incident changes the protagonist's world in a dramatic way, the lead-up must help make the inciting incident believable.

Inciting Incident (Reminder)

The main event in the inciting incident hints at the story goal written in your skeleton blurb. The event is not strong enough yet to motivate the protagonist to accept the story goal. But it does shake up their world.

Reaction to the Inciting Incident

For the story to have depth, the protagonist must react to the inciting incident. Something has happened to shake up their ordinary world, and it's only natural that they have to react to it. If they don't, then the inciting incident is not strong enough.

Resistance to the Story Goal

Between the inciting incident and plot point 1, the protagonist will resist the story goal. This will add tension to Act 1.

Lead-Up to Plot Point 1

The scene right before plot point 1 is the last time the protagonist resists the story goal. Plot point 1 is when the protagonist accepts the story goal, so the lead-up must help make that event believable.

Your Fun Outlining Task

This one is easy.

Add the following scene names which are in bold to your outline. We're going to create a main event for each of these new scenes in the next section. You'll create the main event for your scenes along with us.

- **Opening image**
- **Lead-up to the inciting incident**
- Inciting incident
- **Reaction to inciting incident**
- **Resistance to story goal**
- **Lead-up to plot point 1**
- Plot point 1

This is the minimum list of scenes needed in Act 1. Every story is unique, and if yours needs more scenes, please do add them. By following how we create the main event for each of the scenes listed above, you'll learn how to create the main event for any scene you need.

Where to Next?

We've taken you from the opening image through to the end of Act 1. Next, you'll outline each scene in Act 1. As we go through this, we'll show you how we outlined *Evolution* and *My Fairy Assassin*.

After that, we look at the first half of Act 2. Act 2 is a biggie, and our philosophy is to create an outline in small steps. We'll show you how to do this.

The Opening Image

The opening image is where the reader meets the story world.

The opening image must:

1. Introduce the protagonist.
2. Show the reader the story world.
3. Show what's at stake for the protagonist.
4. Show the tone of the story.

The main event in the opening scene must match the tone of the rest of the story. If the opening scene is all lighthearted, and the story is about a harrowing experience, the reader will feel the opening image was not relevant to the rest of the story.

If there is a prologue, the opening image happens in the prologue. A prologue must be relevant to the story.

When you outline your story, refer to your skeleton blurb. This shows the story goal and the story stakes.

Evolution

The skeleton blurb for *Evolution* is:

> **Jaz Cooper must find out who killed her husband using her ability to see into a dog's mind; otherwise, she might die.**

Because we've already outlined the five story arc scenes, we know that the dog visions don't come into play until the inciting incident, so we can't use that in the opening image. This must show Jaz in her ordinary world without the ability to see into a dog's mind.

What we know for *Evolution* is that Jaz's husband is dead. We've decided this makes her question whether life is worth living. We're going to start the story by showing the reader how Jaz behaves at her husband's funeral. We want to isolate Jaz, so she struggles alone.

We decided the main event in the **opening image** is:

> **Jaz abandons her family and bolts from her husband's funeral.**

My Fairy Assassin

My Fairy Assassin is a young adult (YA) fantasy novel, so in the opening image, the protagonist's present-day world must be explored.

We know Liv's world will come tumbling down when she learns she must save her sister's life, so for the first image we want to show the world is broken for both the environment and the relationships that she has left.

The skeleton blurb is:

> **Liv Wright must use the fairy time portal to save her fairy assassin sister; otherwise, a scientist will destroy the world.**

We want to show Liv's world is falling apart. This puts pressure on her and adds tension to Act I. It establishes the stakes early and gets the reader to worry.

We decided the main event in the **opening image** is:

> **Liv's world, the eco-ark, is falling apart.**

Here you can see how the opening image shows Liv in her world that is collapsing. Her ordinary world is in a desperate state, and this will drive her to make it better. We've shown that 'what' and not the 'how' for now. We'll get to how the world is falling apart during the draft phase.

Your Fun Outlining Task

The opening image will be the first scene in your novel the reader reads.

Create the main event and make sure the event sets up the scene, so you can:
1. Introduce the protagonist.
2. Show the reader the story world.
3. Show what's at stake for the protagonist.
4. Show the tone of the story.

You don't have to know the details yet. When you write the draft, you'll fill in those details. For now, you want the outline to set you up to easily write every scene in the first draft.

You may decide to add a prologue later, but for now outline a scene that introduces the protagonist. You can build the story around that.

If you're having difficulty determining what the main event for the opening image is, try defining a main event for what the protagonist was doing right before the opening scene. This will help you determine the main event for the opening image. You don't need to include the lead-up to the opening image in the outline if it's not going to be included in the story. The purpose is to help you see what emotional state the protagonist is in before the story starts.

For some writers, the main event in the opening image isn't clear to them until they know what the closing image is. When that happens, add a scene to your outline called Opening Image and come back to the main event later.

Where to Next?

Let's look at what main event should go into the lead-up to the inciting incident.

Lead-Up to the Inciting Incident

The main event in the lead-up to the inciting incident is important as it will show the reader what's at stake for the protagonist.

As we stated earlier, this scene can be part of the opening image and/or the inciting incident scene if the inciting incident is the first scene in the story. If that's true, outline them as separate scenes and then combine them. This will show you the story structure and ensure you don't miss key parts of the story.

The main event in this scene must show the reader why the story goal will be important to the protagonist.

This scene will show the reader what will happen if the protagonist does not go after the story goal. There might be hints of everything carrying on the same and the protagonist being unhappy with their lot. Or there could be hints of how bleak the future will be. There can be hints that the protagonist may or may not survive if they don't take on the story goal.

This scene is the setup for the inciting incident. When you outline this scene, look at what must happen to make the main event in the inciting incident scene believable.

If you think about the scene before the meet-cute scene in a romance novel, what will make the story message stronger? Has the protagonist sworn off getting a partner? Has the protagonist had a gift of a rather unfortunate ugly Christmas jumper, and she wears it to the party where she will meet her future partner, like in *Bridget Jones's Diary*? The lead-up to the inciting incident is about making sure the inciting incident has greater meaning to the reader.

Remember: The scene right before the inciting incident is the last time the protagonist will experience their ordinary world. The inciting incident changes the protagonist's world in a dramatic way.

Evolution

Here is what we have so far for *Evolution*:

Skeleton blurb: Jaz Cooper must find out who killed her husband using her ability to see into a dog's mind; otherwise, she might die.

Opening Image: Jaz abandons her family and bolts from her husband's funeral.

Inciting Incident: Jaz saves a dog's life and gains the ability to see into the dog's mind.

Plot Point 1: Jaz uses a dog vision and finally believes her husband was murdered.

Middle Plot Point: Jaz sees a new dog vision. She misinterprets the vision, and it leads her on the wrong path to finding her husband's killer.

Plot Point 2: Jaz's action causes someone close to her to die.

Climax: Using a dog's vision, Jaz discovers who murdered her husband.

In Jaz's ordinary world, her husband recently died. She doesn't know yet his death was not an accident. All she knows is she is alone and depressed. The inciting incident is going to jar her out of this depression.

We decided the main event in the **lead-up to the inciting incident** is:

> **Jaz is alone at home and suicidal.**

This main event is important because it sets up that the story goal of finding out who killed her husband is going to keep her from being suicidal.

My Fairy Assassin

The inciting incident needs some preparation, be it a page in the first chapter, or a scene all by itself. The lead-up to the inciting incident shows how important the inciting incident scene is.

Here's what we have so far for *My Fairy Assassin*.

The skeleton blurb is Liv Wright must use the fairy time portal to save her fairy assassin sister; otherwise, a scientist will destroy the world.

Inciting Incident: Liv discovers her sister is not dead yet but stuck in a time portal.

We know in the inciting incident Liv finds out her sister is not dead. This means in the lead-up to the inciting incident, she must think she is dead; otherwise, the inciting incident doesn't make sense.

We decided the main event in the **lead-up to the inciting incident** is:

> **Liv finds out her sister is missing and presumed dead.**

This main event is important because it sets up the story goal of using the fairy time portal to save her fairy assassin sister. She'll be so relieved her sister is not dead that she must act.

Your Fun Outlining Task

You know your skeleton blurb. You know the main event in the inciting incident. Review the scenes you've already outlined.

Refer to:

- Your skeleton blurb.
- The main event in the inciting incident.
- The scenes you've already outlined.

Ask yourself what could happen in the lead-up to the inciting incident to cause the main event in the inciting incident. Here you are looking for an action that causes a reaction. What is connecting the two scenes?

1. Use all of this to list the main event for the lead-up to the inciting incident as we have for **Evolution** and **My Fairy Assassin**.

The main event must make sense in the context of the other scenes. Every time you add a new main event, you may have to alter the existing ones. That's OK. It's all part of the process.

Where to Next?

You have outlined the lead-up to the inciting incident and the inciting incident. Next, we'll outline the protagonist's reaction to the inciting incident.

Reaction to the Inciting Incident

> **This scene shows how the protagonist reacts to the main event in the inciting incident.**

The inciting incident is the moment the protagonist's world changes in a dramatic way, so it's an action scene.

Let's look at what we have so far.
- You've already outlined the lead-up to the inciting incident, so you know what's at stake for the protagonist.
- You've outlined the inciting incident, so you know what happened to change the protagonist's world.
- You know the main event in the five story arc scenes, so you where the story is going.

You have the knowledge you need to outline the reaction to the inciting incident.

While the inciting incident should be an action scene, the reaction to the inciting incident is better suited to a sequel scene, as this will add depth to the reader's understanding of the story. This depth is why readers connect with stories. Reading is a time someone can be inside another's mind, and this engages readers. We all want to know how others think.

A sequel scene (a reaction to a main event in a previous scene) must still have a main action in it, so let's look at how to show this.

The main event in a sequel scene is about a character's reaction to a previous event.

You showed the stakes when you outlined the lead-up to the inciting incident. This scene shows how far the protagonist must go to be successful.

If we think about the reaction to meeting Mr. Darcy in *Pride and Prejudice* and having him dismiss Elizabeth Bennet, then in a following scene, Elizabeth says she will never dance with Mr. Darcy. And right there, we fall in love with misguided Elizabeth and hope Mr. Darcy can be worthy of her.

Evolution

In the main event in the reaction to the inciting incident scene, we define what happens right after the inciting incident. We're going to use this information later to determine the best starting point for the story.

We need our blurb: Jaz Cooper must find out who killed her husband using her ability to see into a dog's mind; otherwise, she might die.

The main event for the inciting incident is Jaz saves a dog's life and gains the ability to see into the dog's mind.

This shows us we need to bring together the dog visions and her husband's death. Right after the inciting incident, Jaz gets her first dog vision but doesn't believe it. The vision hints that her husband was killed.

We decided the main event in the **reaction to inciting incident** is:

> **Jaz's first vision hints at her husband's murder.**

To be successful, Jaz must accept her husband was murdered and didn't die in an accident.

My Fairy Assassin

My Fairy Assassin's skeleton blurb: Liv Wright must use the fairy time portal to save her fairy assassin sister; otherwise, a scientist will destroy the world.

Lead-up to the Inciting Incident: Liv finds out her sister is missing and presumed dead.

Inciting Incident: Liv discovers her sister is not dead yet but is stuck in a dying fairy world.

Plot Point 1: Liv's sister is dying, and Liv must learn to time travel to save her.

Middle Plot Point: Liv time travels to save her sister.

Plot Point 2: The time portal fails, and Liv cannot save her sister.

Climax: Liv saves her sister by reopening the time portal and injuring the scientist.

In the inciting incident, Liv learns that her sister is stuck in a time portal. The obvious reaction is that Liv must find her, and to do that, she must time travel. The only way to time travel is through the fairy world.

We decided the **reaction to inciting incident** is:

> **Liv enters the fairy world to save her sister.**

Your Fun Outlining Task

We're back to making the list for our outline. To spark your imagination, refer to:

- Your skeleton blurb.
- The main event for the opening image. This is important because it shows you the ordinary world and will help you decide the protagonist's reaction to the change in the world.
- The main event for the inciting incident.

With this, you have the knowledge you need, and it's time for you to figure out the main event for the reaction to the inciting incident.

So, yes, your fun outlining task is:
1. Create the main event for the reaction to the inciting incident scene.
2. Place that scene right after the inciting incident in your outline.

Where to Next?

You now have an inciting incident sequence that will flow, creating a strong structure from which you can launch a story.

With change comes resistance. So next, we're going to outline the scene where the protagonist resists the story goal.

Resistance to the story goal

For Act 1, we've already outlined:

- Lead-up to the inciting incident.
- The inciting incident.
- Reaction to the inciting incident.

Now, it's time to increase the tension in the story. To do this, the protagonist must resist the story goal. In the inciting incident, their world changed in a dramatic way, and they didn't like it. Now, they must show resistance to the change.

In a romance, this scene is where the protagonist decides the romantic interest is the last person they would ever be with.

In a murder mystery, like *Evolution*, this is the scene where Jaz refuses to see that her husband's death might have been murder instead of an accident.

To outline the main event in the Resistance to the Story Goal, we need:

- The skeleton blurb.
- The inciting incident.
- The main event in the reaction to the inciting incident scenes.

These three items alone give us enough information to create the main event for this scene.

Evolution

Evolution's Skeleton Blurb

Jaz Cooper must find out who killed her husband using her ability to see into a dog's mind; otherwise, she might die.

Inciting Incident:

Jaz saves a dog's life and gains the ability to see into the dog's mind.

Main event in the reaction to the inciting incident:

Jaz's first vision hints at her husband's murder.

The dog visions hint that Jaz's husband has been murdered, but Jaz refused to believe them. We will need a sequence of scenes to increase the importance of the dog visions.

We decided the **resistance to the story goal** is:

Jaz resists believing her husband was murdered.

Wasn't that easy?

My Fairy Assassin

My Fairy Assassin's Skeleton Blurb:

Liv Wright must use the fairy time portal to save her fairy assassin sister; otherwise, a scientist will destroy the world.

Inciting Incident:

Liv discovers her sister is not dead yet but is stuck in a dying fairy world.

Reaction to the Inciting Incident:

Liv enters the fairy world to save her sister.

Liv is now in the fairy world she knows nothing about. She doesn't know where to find her sister but knows she must. She's lost and alone.

We decided the **resistance to story goal** is:

> **Liv resists believing she is capable of changing things.**

Your Fun Outlining Task

You're probably getting the hang of this by now, however, we'll continue to make this easy for you. We're going to list the steps.

1. Refer to your skeleton blurb.
2. Refer to your inciting incident.
3. Refer to the main event for the reaction to the inciting incident scene.
4. Create the main event in the resistance to the story scene.
5. Add a new scene to your outline called 'Resistance to the Story Goal.'

Please do this before you continue reading. Each step is built on the previous step.

Where to Next?

The tension is rising, so let's keep this going. The next scene to outline is the lead-up to plot point 1. In plot point 1, the protagonist accepts the story goal. It's your job as the writer to figure out how you're going to get them to do this.

Lead-Up to Plot Point 1

It's worth repeating what we've outlined. So far, we know the main events for the following scenes in Act 1.

- Opening image
- Lead-up to the inciting incident

- Inciting incident
- Reaction to the inciting incident
- Resistance to the story goal
- Plot point 1

The lead-up to plot point 1 is going to go right between the resistance to the story goal and plot point 1. You can see by now how important it was to outline the story arc scenes before outlining other scenes in the story. The story arc scenes create the spine of the story. Everything we outlined is related to that spine. We're setting you up, so every scene in your story will relate to the story goal.

You know what the ordinary world is and what's at stake for the protagonist. You know what happened that changed their ordinary world in the inciting incident. You also know what the main event in plot point 1 is. This means you're starting with a firm knowledge base.

The goal now is to decide what the main event is in the scene prior to plot point 1. The protagonist still hasn't accepted the story goal, and this scene is their last chance to walk away from the goal. If there is any way the protagonist can do this, they will. You must make sure you set up the protagonist to accept the goal, or the story is over.

When outlining this scene, look to see what would lead the protagonist to accept the story goal in plot point 1.

To create a main event for the lead-up to plot point 1, review the scenes you've outlined so far that come before plot point 1.

Evolution

For *Evolution*, we used the following:

Evolution's Skeleton Blurb:

Jaz Cooper must find out who killed her husband using her ability to see into a dog's mind; otherwise, she might die.

Reaction to the Inciting Incident:

Jaz's first vision hints at her husband's murder.

Resistance to the Story Goal :

Jaz resists believing her husband was murdered.

Plot Point 1 is:

Jaz uses a dog vision and finally believes her husband was murdered.

Before we get to plot point 1, we need a scene to show Jaz preparing for plot point 1. For plot point 1 to be believable, we need a scene showing Jaz proof the visions are real.

We decided the main event in the **lead-up to plot point 1** is:

Jaz believes the dog visions are real.

This works for us because believing the visions are real will lead Jaz to believe her husband was murdered. She'll stop resisting this truth.

My Fairy Assassin

For *My Fairy Assassin* we used:

My Fairy Assassin's Skeleton Blurb:

Liv Wright must use the fairy time portal to save her fairy assassin sister; otherwise, a scientist will destroy the world.

Lead-Up to the Inciting Incident:

Liv finds out her sister is missing and presumed dead.

Inciting Incident:

Liv discovers her sister is not dead yet but is stuck in a dying fairy world.

Reaction to the Inciting Incident:

Liv enters the fairy world to save her sister.

Resistance to the Story Goal:

Liv resists believing she is capable of changing things.

Plot Point 1:

Liv must learn how to use the time portal.

To do this, she must trust what she learns from the fairies. Liv won't have the confidence to time travel if she doesn't have some skills to support her.

We decided the **lead-up to plot point 1** is:

> **Liv starts to see the fairy rules are ones that need following.**

Your Fun Outlining Task

It's time again to use the work you've already done. Refer to:

- The skeleton blurb.
- The story goal.
- The story stakes.
- The main events you've outlined so far.

Your fun tasks are:

1. Decide what the main event in the lead-up to plot point 1 scene is.
2. Add it to the rest of the scenes you've already outlined.

You can read our outlines for *Evolution* and *My Fairy Assassin* in the last two sections of this chapter. We're doing this to keep focused on the story we want to tell. We're also doing this to see how far we've come.

Where to Next?

You're amazing. You've outlined Act 1. Before we move on to outlining the first half of Act 2, we're going to show you our outlines for *Evolution* and *My Fairy Assassin*. These outlines show the theory we've presented via examples.

Evolution Act 1

Here we see Act 1 outlined for *Evolution*. We are listing the main event in each scene in Act 1 plus the story arc scenes. This is not the full list of scenes that will be in the final version of the story.

The outline is giving us a structure to write within. It will test our imagination. It will force us to be creative. And it will keep us from writing a story that doesn't work.

Skeleton Blurb:

Jaz Cooper must find out who killed her husband using her ability to see into a dog's mind; otherwise, she might die.

Opening Image:

Jaz abandons her family and bolts from her husband's funeral.

Lead-Up to the Inciting Incident:

Jaz is alone at home and suicidal.

Inciting Incident:

Jaz saves a dog's life and gains the ability to see into the dog's mind.

Reaction to the Inciting Incident:

Jaz's first dog vision hints at her husband's murder.

Resistance to the Story Goal:

Jaz resists believing her husband was murdered.

Lead-Up to Plot Point 1:

Jaz believes the dog visions are real.

Plot Point 1:

Jaz uses a dog vision and finally believes her husband was murdered.

Middle Plot Point:

Jaz sees a new dog vision. She misinterprets the vision, and it leads her on the wrong path to finding her husband's killer.

Plot Point 2:

Jaz's action causes someone close to her to die.

Climax:

Using a dog's vision, Jaz discovers who murdered her husband.

My Fairy Assassin Act 1

In this section, we see Act 1 outlined for *My Fairy Assassin*. We are listing the main event in each scene in Act 1 plus the story arc scenes.

This is not the full list of scenes that will be in the final version of the story.

As with *Evolution*, the outline is giving us a structure to write within. It will test our imagination. It will force us to be creative. And it will keep us from writing a story that doesn't work.

Skeleton Blurb:

Liv Wright must use the fairy time portal to save her fairy assassin sister; otherwise, a scientist will destroy the world.

Opening Image:

Liv's world, the eco-ark, is falling apart.

Lead-Up to the Inciting Incident:

Liv finds out her sister is missing and presumed dead.

Inciting Incident:

Liv discovers her sister is not dead yet but is stuck in a dying fairy world.

Reaction to the Inciting Incident:

Liv enters the fairy world to save her sister.

Resistance to the Story Goal:

Liv resists believing she is capable of changing things.

Lead-Up to Plot Point 1:

Liv starts to see the fairy rules are ones that need following.

Plot Point 1:

Liv's sister is dying, and Liv must learn to time travel to save her.

Middle Plot Point:

Liv time travels to save sister.

Plot Point 2:

The time portal fails, and Liv cannot save her sister.

Climax:

Liv saves her sister by reopening the time portal and injuring the scientist.

Chapter Seven: Outlining the First Half of Act 2

You'll recall Act 2 kicks off the story, increases conflict, and shows the story's theme.

Every main event we add in Act 2 will make it difficult for the protagonist to achieve the story goal stated in the skeleton blurb. Everything we outline here will support the Act 2 requirements.

Act 2 must:
1. Keep the reader reading the novel.
2. Show there is more than the reader initially thought about the story world.
3. Show there is more than the reader initially thought about relationships between the characters.
4. Show there is more than the reader initially thought to the depth of the plot.
5. Have failures and successes that propel the reader through this section of the book.

Act 2 makes up fifty percent of the story. To make outlining easier, we are going to break Act 2 into two halves. In this chapter, we'll outline the first half of Act 2. This includes the scenes from plot point 1 to the scene right before the middle plot point.

Lucky for us, we've already listed the main events for plot point 1 and the middle plot point, so we have a structure to work from.

Note that it's not important whether you place plot point 1 at the end of Act 1 or the start of Act 2. It's a transition scene from Act 1 to Act 2. The function remains the same regardless of what act you include the scene in.

Every scene must lead to the next scene. It must feel natural to the reader. This means the scenes connecting the acts, making the story flow, are vital.

We've already listed the main event for plot point 1, and now we are going to use it to kick off Act 2.

Now that you've outlined Act 1, confirm the main event in plot point 1 is something the protagonist cannot turn away from. If the protagonist can turn away from the story goal, it's time to redefine the main event in plot point 1. We strongly recommend you do this before outlining the first half of Act 2.

Accepting the story goal must be addressed in the outline. This will build this aspect of plot point 1 deeply into your structure, even if the note to yourself in the outline only states: the protagonist must have no other option than to accept the story goal.

First Half of Act 2

In the first half of Act 2, you'll be increasing the pacing of the story. We're going to show you what scenes to add to the outline to help with this. Act 2 is sometimes seen as a saggy part of the story. But sagginess can be avoided by, you guessed it, knowing what a story needs to increase its structural strength.

Aren't you dying to know what the next scenes are?

First, we need a reaction scene to plot point 1. The reader won't feel satisfied if they don't get to see the protagonist reacting to the main event in plot point 1. The protagonist has just decided to go after the story goal, even though they don't want to. This story arc scene must impact the protagonist, and the reader will want to know how.

The impact on the protagonist is part of the vicarious nature of reading. We readers love to understand how the events affect the protagonist's internal life. How do they feel about the events happening around them? Readers can be empathetic because they gain insights into how humans react to powerful events.

The outline also must set up the story, so it's easy for you to add conflict and tension to scenes when you're writing the first draft. Conflict and tension increase pacing.

It's time to refer to your story blurb again.

We must outline how it's going to be difficult for the protagonist to achieve the story goal, so we need three attempts at the story goal before the middle plot point. Let's make your protagonist work hard to get what they want. A protagonist who works hard is interesting.

After the goal attempts, we need one more scene called the lead-up to the middle plot point.

This gives us the scenes we need to outline in the first half of Act 2.

First Half of Act 2 Outline

1. Plot point 1
2. Reaction to plot point 1
3. Goal attempt 1
4. Goal attempt 2
5. Goal attempt 3
6. Lead-up to the middle plot point

These scenes are going to get us to the middle plot point, where you discover the choice the protagonist makes that takes them farther away from the story goal even if they think it will bring them closer.

You can see what we're doing here. When you take an enormous task and break it into smaller tasks, it's not overwhelming. It becomes fun. The excitement of making progress on a novel will keep you motivated. You will write AND finish this novel.

Your Fun Outlining Task

We're really making progress now. Before reading on, here are your fun tasks.
1. Check that the main event in plot point 1 is strong enough, and the scene works with the scenes you outlined for Act 1.
2. Add the five scenes (in bold in the list below) to your outline.

To recap, the story outline we've built so far is:

- Opening Image
- Lead-Up to the Inciting Incident
- Inciting Incident
- Reaction to the Inciting Incident
- Resistance to the Story Goal
- Lead-Up to Plot Point 1
- Plot Point 1
- **Reaction to Plot Point 1**
- **Goal Attempt 1**
- **Goal Attempt 2**
- **Goal Attempt 3**
- **Lead-Up to the Middle Plot Point**
- Middle Plot Point
- Plot Point 2
- Climax
- Resolution

Where to Next?

Your story structure is getting stronger, so keep going. Let's get the first half of Act 2 outlined.

We'll start with the reaction to plot point 1.

Reaction to Plot Point 1

Outlining is making sure you have the right mix of the actions and reactions that the reader will subconsciously expect in a story. When we come to use our outline, sometimes we can get distracted by the exciting action scenes and forget the reaction scenes are the reason those action scenes can shine. Reaction scenes are the structural equivalent of the settings needed for a diamond necklace.

Chapter Seven: Outlining The First Half Of Act 2

Skeleton Blurb Time

It's time for a reminder of the skeleton blurb. Pull yours out now and read it. You'll also need to remind yourself of what the main events in the lead-up to plot point 1 and plot point 1 are.

Evolution

The Skeleton Blurb for *Evolution* is:

Jaz Cooper must find out who killed her husband using her ability to see into a dog's mind; otherwise, she might die.

The main event in the lead-up to plot point 1 is:

Jaz believes the dog visions are real.

The main event in plot point 1 is:

Jaz uses a dog vision and finally believes her husband was murdered.

We can see plot point 1 is where Jaz decides to go after the story goal: find out who killed her husband using her ability to see into a dog's mind.

There are two choices for the reaction to plot point 1. One is to make the reaction to plot point 1 heavy on action. Two is to make the scene heavy on reaction. The choice you make will depend on the genre and type of story you're writing.

The dog visions are important to the story, so we think they should be part of Jaz's reaction. In the scene right before plot point 1, Jaz received proof the dog visions show actual events. She's had two big discoveries in a row, and this indicates the reader might need a breather.

For *Evolution*, we decided to make this scene heavy on reaction because learning her husband has been murdered when she thought his death was an accident requires a reaction. Learning that what she sees in a dog's mind are actual events also requires a reaction.

We know at the middle plot point, Jaz misinterprets a dog vision, and that takes her on the wrong path.

We also know in plot point 2, Jaz's action causes someone close to her to die.

The story needs to foreshadow the middle plot point and plot point 2, but not show the events of those scenes. Something in the dog vision in plot point 1 will trigger Jaz to search for clues.

In the reaction to plot point 1, while she's searching, she'll also be reacting to what she's recently learned. This gives us a way to keep Jaz in motion during a scene that's heavy on reaction.

The main event for the reaction to plot point 1 is:

> **Jaz reacts internally to her husband being murdered and searches for clues.**

My Fairy Assassin

The Skeleton Blurb for *My Fairy Assassin* is:

Liv Wright must use the fairy time portal to save her fairy assassin sister; otherwise, a scientist will destroy the world.

The Main Event in the Lead-Up to Plot Point 1 is:

Liv starts to see the fairy rules are ones that need following.

The Main Event in Plot Point 1 is:

Liv's sister is dying, and Liv must learn to time travel to save her.

In Act 1, we set up the ordinary world, we gave the reader time to connect with the protagonist, and the protagonist has accepted the story goal. Liv is going to need help achieving that goal, and there will be characters who get in her way. This means the first half of Act 2 is a great place to add supporting characters. We know Liv must be feeling frightened and alone because her sister is dying, and she doesn't know how to save her. It seems natural her reaction would be to find help. We decided Liv needs a partner to help her navigate time traveling.

The main event for the **reaction to plot point 1** is:

> **Liv must choose a fairy time travel partner, who shows her she must pass three tests in order to time travel.**

Your Fun Outlining Task

Follow the process we used above for *Evolution* and *My Fairy Assassin* to:
1. Create the main event you need for your protagonist to react to in plot point 1.
2. Add the scene to your outline.

We used the following to help us determine the **reaction to plot point 1**:

- The skeleton blurb
- The main event in the lead-up to plot point 1
- The main event in plot point 1
- The main event in the middle plot point
- The main event in plot point 2

You're going deeper into your story outline and making decisions about your story. This is an iterative process. At any point, you may go back and update earlier scene events. This is part of the process. Later, we'll show an example of where this happened for *Evolution*.

Where to Next?

After you know how your protagonist reacts to plot point 1, it's time for them to try to achieve the main story goal. They'll fail, of course; otherwise, the story is over.

The Goal Attempts

The goal attempts are different ways the protagonist tries to reach the story goal listed in the skeleton blurb. All you need to do at this point is list three ways the protagonist tries to reach their goal. Don't get stuck here. You can change these later if you need to.

Our goal is to complete the outline, then come back and ensure each main event is doing its job.

What's important is all three goal attempts are different. The protagonist must not try the same thing three times. The reader will get bored with this.

One guiding pattern is to have two of the goal attempts fail and one succeed. This will create tension and conflict, yet still give the reader a sense of hope.

Evolution

In *Evolution*, Jaz has reacted to plot point 1 and is searching for clues. One place to go is to have her use one of the clues to try to find out who murdered her husband. We need the middle plot point and plot point 2.

Middle Plot Point: Jaz sees a new dog vision. She misinterprets the vision, and it leads her on the wrong path to finding her husband's killer.

Plot Point 2: Jaz's actions cause someone close to her to die.

We decided the main event in **goal attempt 1** is:

> **Jaz uses a clue found in the reaction to plot point 1 and fails to solve her husband's murder. She won't use dog visions in this attempt.**

Did you notice we ignored part of the story goal in the blurb for *Evolution*? The blurb states: Jaz Cooper must find out who killed her husband using **her ability to see into a dog's mind**; otherwise, she might die.

She didn't use the dog visions, so this goal must fail.

Now, she's frustrated and searches for new ways to find her husband's murderer. At this point in the story, she doesn't have any clear suspects, so how about we have Jaz get to know people her husband worked with or hung out with? Jaz can pet their dogs and see into their lives.

We decided the main event in **goal attempt 2** is:

> **With the help of a friend, Jaz uses a dog vision to search for her husband's killer and fails.**

By involving others in her quest, she puts those she loves in danger. This foreshadows plot point 2 where she loses a friend.

So now, she's tried the normal way to search for clues. She's tried to find her husband's murderer using just dog visions. It's time to combine the two.

We decided the main event in **goal attempt 3** is:

> **Jaz reacts to an event and combines traditional investigative methods with dog visions to search for her husband's killer.**

She gets one step closer to finding the killer. Jaz gains confidence in her ability to use the dog visions, and this foreshadows the middle plot point where Jaz misinterprets a dog vision, and that takes her on the wrong path. She's overconfident in the middle plot point.

We've built the attempts to show Jaz's skills improving, but also to show she's still reacting to events and not proactively searching for her husband's killer. We'll make her proactive at the middle plot point.

The main events for these three scenes are:

Goal Attempt 1: Jaz uses a clue found in reaction to plot point 1 and fails to solve her husband's murder. She won't use dog visions in this attempt.

Goal Attempt 2: With the help of a friend, Jaz uses a dog vision to search for her husband's killer and fails.

Goal Attempt 3: Jaz reacts to an event and combines traditional investigative methods with dog visions to search for her husband's killer.

Here you can see Jaz tried two approaches and failed. One approach used traditional investigative skills, and the second used only the dog visions. The third attempt moves her closer to her goal because she combined the skills. This is a learning moment for Jaz.

My Fairy Assassin

In *My Fairy Assassin*, Liv must pass three tests. Each test binds her closer to the fairy she chose in the reaction to plot point 1.

We decided the main event in **goal attempt 1** is:

> **The maze test. This is based on the idea that humans lose all sense of direction, and only if she can get through the maze will she survive.**

We decided the main event in **goal attempt 2** is:

> **The arrows test. If Liv gets the straightest arrow, she will get the power to choose who she will bond with.**

We decided the main event in **goal attempt 3** is:

> **The truth test: Liv misunderstands the Salmon of Truth and thinks she's failed the test.**

We're building up to the middle plot point where Liv will move from reactive to proactive.

Your Fun Outlining Task

Think about the different ways your protagonist can try to achieve the story goal. This is about the three little pigs, and how they keep building a stronger and stronger house, so the antagonist does not win. Your fun tasks are:

1. Refer to the following from your outline:

- Your skeleton blurb
- Main event in plot point 1
- Main event in the middle plot point
- Main event in plot point 2

2. Use these to create the main event for each of the three goal attempts that:

- Foreshadow the middle plot point.
- Foreshadow plot point 2.
- Show your protagonist reacting to events of previous scenes.
- Show two of the three attempts failing. Show one of the events leading them in the right direction but NOT achieving the story goal.

3. Add all three goal attempts to your outline.

If you can't come up with three goal attempts now, don't worry. Just list the main event as: Goal Attempt X. You can come back to this later when you have more of the story outlined. You may also find you add more goal attempts. Later in this book, we'll help you outline each of the story arc scenes in detail. This may give you ideas for any scenes you had trouble with.

Where to Next?

We have one more scene to outline before we can move on to the second half of Act 2. You've already outlined the middle plot point, and before that, there must be a scene leading up to the middle plot point. Let's get to it.

Lead-Up to the Middle Plot Point

The goal of this scene is to build up to the middle plot point where the protagonist moves from a reactionary state to a proactive state.

At this point in the story, the protagonist is feeling frustrated because they've tried to achieve their goal three times, and they still haven't achieved the story goal.

The goal attempts help you decide what the main event for the **lead-up to the middle plot point** scene is.

Evolution

Let's start with what we know.

The Skeleton Blurb for *Evolution* is:

Jaz Cooper must find out who killed her husband using her ability to see into a dog's mind; otherwise, she might die.

Plot Point 1:

Jaz uses a dog vision and finally believes her husband was murdered.

Reaction to Plot Point 1:

Jaz reacts internally to her husband being murdered and searches for clues.

Goal Attempt 1:

Jaz uses a clue found in the reaction to plot point 1 and fails. She won't use dog visions in this attempt.

Goal Attempt 2:

With the help of a friend, Jaz uses a dog vision to search for her husband's killer and fails.

Goal Attempt 3:

Jaz reacts to an event and combines traditional investigative methods with dog visions to search for her husband's killer.

Middle Plot Point:

Jaz sees a new dog vision. She misinterprets the vision, and it leads her on the wrong path to finding her husband's killer.

This information helps us determine the main event for the scene right before the middle plot point.

In the next scene, the middle plot point, Jaz is going to take a wrong path because of a dog vision. This means this scene must show her using a dog vision successfully, so she trusts the visions in the next scene. You can see how we're using the outline to figure out what each scene must accomplish.

We decided the main event in the **lead-up to the middle plot point** is:

> **Jaz uses a dog vision and finds a clue. She celebrates she can now use the visions to find out who killed her husband.**

My Fairy Assassin

The Skeleton Blurb for *My Fairy Assassin* is:

Liv Wright must use the fairy time portal to save her fairy assassin sister; otherwise, a scientist will destroy the world.

Plot Point 1:

Liv's sister is dying, and Liv must learn to time travel to save her.

The Main Event for the Reaction to Plot Point 1:

Liv must choose a fairy time travel partner, who shows her she must pass three tests in order to time travel.

Goal Attempt 1:

The maze test. This is based on the idea that humans lose all sense of direction, and only if she can get through the maze will she survive.

Goal Attempt 2:

The arrows test. If Liv gets the straightest arrow, she will get the power to choose who she will bond with.

Goal Attempt 3:

The truth test. Liv misunderstands the Salmon of Truth and thinks she's failed the test.

Middle Plot Point:

Liv time travels.

This information helps us determine the main event for the scene right before the middle plot point.

In the next scene, the middle plot point, Liv must be dressed appropriately in order to time travel through the portal, so she does not stand out in the time period she's going to. The clothes signify the new Liv.

We decided the main event in the **lead-up to the middle plot point** is:

> **Getting dressed to time travel.**

Your Fun Outlining Task

Let's get specific and actionable.
For your outline, refer to the following:
- Your skeleton blurb
- Plot point 1
- Reaction to plot point 1
- Goal attempt 1
- Goal attempt 2
- Goal attempt 3
- Lead-up to the middle plot point
- Middle plot point

The fun tasks are:
1. Use these to list the main event in the scene leading up to the middle plot point.
2. Add the new scene to your outline.

Where to Next?

We're done outlining the first half of Act 2, and it's time to outline the second half of the novel. We need to complete the outline for Act 2 before we can move on to Act 3.

Before the next chapter, we'll show where we are with the outline for *Evolution* and *My Fairy Assassin*. Review our outlines together with your outline before moving to the second half of Act 2.

Evolution Outline

We are growing our story outline and adding depth to it, while at the same time giving ourselves freedom to be creative during drafting.

Here is what we have so far for *Evolution*. Keep in mind we can come back at any time and change the outline.

Opening Image:

Jaz abandons her family and bolts from her husband's funeral.

Lead-Up to the Inciting Incident:

Jaz is at home feeling suicidal.

Inciting Incident:

Jaz saves a dog's life and gains the ability to see into the dog's mind.

Reaction to the Inciting Incident:

Jaz's first dog vision hints at her husband's murder.

Resistance to the Story Goal:

Jaz resists believing her husband was murdered.

Lead-Up to Plot Point 1:

Jaz believes the dog visions are real.

Plot Point 1:

Jaz uses a dog vision and finally believes her husband was murdered.

Reaction to Plot Point 1:

Jaz reacts internally to her husband being murdered and searches for clues.

Goal Attempt 1:

Jaz uses a clue found in reaction to plot point 1 and fails. She won't use dog visions in this attempt.

Goal Attempt 2:

With the help of a friend, Jaz uses a dog vision to search for her husband's killer and fails.

Goal Attempt 3:

Jaz reacts to an event and combines traditional investigative methods with dog visions to search for her husband's killer.

Lead-Up to the Middle Plot Point:

Jaz uses a dog vision and finds a clue. She celebrates she can now use the visions to find out who killed her husband.

Middle Plot Point:

Jaz sees a new dog vision. She misinterprets the vision, and it leads her on the wrong path to finding her husband's killer.

Plot Point 2:

Jaz's actions cause someone close to her to die.

Climax:

Using a dog's vision, Jaz discovers who killed her husband.

Where to Next?

Let's see how far along we are in *My Fairy Assassin*.

My Fairy Assassin Outline

Opening Image:

Liv's world, the eco-ark, is falling apart.

Lead-Up to the Inciting Incident:

Liv finds out her sister is missing and presumed dead.

Inciting Incident:

Liv discovers her sister is not dead yet but is stuck in a dying fairy world.

Reaction to the Inciting Incident:

Liv enters the fairy world to save her sister.

Resistance to the Story Goal:

Liv resists believing she is capable of changing things.

Lead-Up to Plot Point 1:

Liv starts to see the fairy rules are ones that need following.

Plot Point 1:

Liv's sister is dying, and Liv must learn to time travel to save her.

Reaction to Plot Point 1:

Liv must choose a fairy time travel partner, who shows her she must pass three tests in order to time travel.

Goal Attempt 1:

The maze test. This is based on the idea that humans lose all sense of direction, and only if she can get through the maze will she survive.

Goal Attempt 2:

The arrows test. If Liv gets the straightest arrow, she will get the power to choose who she will bond with.

Goal Attempt 3:

The truth test: Liv misunderstands the Salmon of Truth and thinks she's failed the test.

Lead-Up to the Middle Plot Point:

Getting dressed to time travel.

Middle Plot Point:

Liv time travels.

Plot Point 2:

The time portal fails, and Liv cannot save her sister.

Climax:

Liv saves her sister by reopening the time portal and injuring the scientist.

Where to Next?

Your story structure is getting stronger, so keep going and let's get the second half of Act 2 outlined.

Chapter Eight: Outlining the Second Half of Act 2

We are on to the second half of Act 2. This means you're halfway through your outline. Brilliant.

You're now going to outline your novel in more depth from the middle plot point to plot point 2. This is the third quarter of your novel.

To fill out the second half of Act 2, here are the new scenes (that are in bold below) to add to the outline.

- Opening Image
- Lead-Up to Indicting Incident
- Inciting Incident
- Reaction to the Inciting Incident
- Resistance to the Story Goal
- Lead-Up to Plot Point 1
- Plot Point 1
- Reaction to Plot Point 1
- Goal Attempt 1
- Goal Attempt 2
- Goal Attempt 3
- Lead-Up to the Middle Plot Point

- Middle Plot Point
- **Reaction to the Middle Plot Point**
- **External Pressure 1**
- **External Pressure 2**
- **External Pressure 3**
- **Lead-Up to Plot Point 2**
- Plot Point 2
- Climax
- Resolution

Let's look at how to create these scenes. As with the previous stages in our outlining process, we'll look at other key scenes to help us figure out what we need in these new scenes.

Your Fun Outlining Task

You're getting there. These are fun scenes to think about because you get to make your protagonist's life difficult.
1. Add the main event for the following five scenes to your outline.

- Reaction to the Middle Plot Point
- External Pressure 1
- External Pressure 2
- External Pressure 3
- Lead-Up to Plot Point 2

Where to Next?

We'll start with the reaction to the middle plot point.

Reaction to the Middle Plot Point

The middle plot point shows the protagonist changing from a reactive state to a proactive state, and the reader will want to see how the protagonist reacts to this change.

This is the first scene in the book where the protagonist actively chases the story goal. Therefore, the reaction should be active. This is not a moment for inner reflection. It's a moment for action.

This shows you the scene following the middle plot point is primarily an action scene and not a sequel.

The reader will want to feel what the protagonist feels, and the emotional reaction can be woven into the action.

Design the main event in the reaction to the middle plot point to give the reader what they need.

Evolution

The Skeleton Blurb for *Evolution* is:

Jaz Cooper must find out who killed her husband using her ability to see into a dog's mind; otherwise, she might die.

The Main Event in the Lead-Up to the Middle Plot Point is:

Jaz uses a dog vision and finds a clue. She celebrates she can now use the visions to find out who killed her husband.

The Main Event in the Middle Plot Point is:

Jaz sees a new dog vision. She misinterprets the vision, and it leads her on the wrong path to finding her husband's killer.

Because Jaz trusts the dog vision based on her success in the lead-up to the middle plot point, she trusts her ability to understand a dog vision.

In the middle plot point, she'll chase the story goal proactively but in the wrong way. This makes for a gripping story.

The dog visions are important to the story, as they are found in the skeleton blurb, so we think they should be part of Jaz's reaction.

Something in the dog vision in the middle plot point triggers Jaz to see the truth but misunderstand what she is seeing. We don't know what the action is yet, so we're going to keep this main event vague.

We decided the main event in the **reaction to the middle plot point** is:

> **Jaz acts on the misunderstanding in the dog vision.**

Here we can see the three scenes working together.

Lead-Up to the Middle Plot Point:

Jaz uses a dog vision and finds a clue. She celebrates she can now use the visions to find out who killed her husband.

Middle Plot Point:

Jaz sees a new dog vision. She misinterprets the vision, and it leads her on the wrong path to finding her husband's killer.

Reaction to the Middle Plot Point:

Jaz acts on the misunderstanding in the dog vision.

My Fairy Assassin

The Skeleton Blurb for *My Fairy Assassin* is:

Liv Wright must use the fairy time portal to save her fairy assassin sister; otherwise, a scientist will destroy the world.

The Lead-Up to the Middle Plot Point is:

Getting dressed to time travel.

The Middle Plot point is:

Liv time travels.

The two preceding scenes are all about getting ready for time travel and then actually time traveling. Liv's goal is to find her sister, so the main event for the reaction to the middle plot becomes obvious.

We decided the main event in the reaction to the **middle plot point** is:

Liv looks for the time lost sister.

You'll have noticed the scene is an action scene. Liv changed from reactive to proactive and now must use action to search for her sister. In the scene, we will show her reaction to successfully time traveling for the first time, but we'll do it throughout the action. She won't have time to stop and think. She must find her sister before her sister dies.

Your Fun Outlining Task

Follow the process we used above for *Evolution* and *My Fairy Assassin* to find the main event you need for your protagonist to react to the middle plot point.

We used the following to help us determine the **reaction to plot point 1**:

- The skeleton blurb.
- The lead-up to the middle plot point.
- The main event in the middle plot point.

1. Create the main event for the reaction to the middle plot point.
2. Add the new scene to your outline right after the middle plot point.

Remember to hold on to the idea that this is an iterative process. You're going deeper into your story outline and making decisions about your story. You might change the main events as you discover your story. That's great. Go for it.

Where to Next?

After you know how your protagonist reacts the middle plot point, it's time for them to try to proactively achieve the main story goal. They'll fail, of course; otherwise, the story is over. We're going to use external pressures to make achieving the story goal harder.

External Pressures

The external pressures are different obstacles the protagonist must face in order reach the story goal stated in the skeleton blurb. All you need to do at this point is list three ways external events make it difficult for the protagonist to reach the story goal. Don't get stuck here. You can change these later if you need to.

Now that the protagonist is proactive instead of reactive, we need to increase the pressure. Every time they act, something must get in their way.

We don't need to figure out all the pressures yet. For now, choose three and add them to your outline. If you can't think of three, for now, add the statement 'External Pressure', so you remember you'll need this scene.

The main event in the middle plot point should foreshadow the pressure. This is a significant piece of information because it will guide you to the best event for the external pressure.

We'll use the main event in the reaction to the middle plot point to help us determine the main event for each of the external pressure scenes.

Not any external pressure will do. The external pressure must be related to the story goal in the skeleton blurb. By now, you're understanding we can't outline without the skeleton blurb. It's the tool we use to keep our outline focused on the story we want to tell.

Chapter Eight: Outlining The Second Half Of Act 2

Let's look at *Evolution* and *My Fairy Assassin*.

Evolution

We need to look at the **reaction to the middle plot point**.

Jaz acts on the misunderstanding in the dog vision.

Because it's the wrong action, Jaz goes down the wrong path. This takes her farther away from reaching her story goal of finding her husband's killer. This leads us to creating external pressures.

Something must happen to threaten Jaz or someone she loves. Perhaps it's a threat to one of her dogs. Or perhaps it's a threat to a friend. This will make her rethink what's she's doing. She'll question whether it's worth the risk.

Jaz has a tight connection to her dogs because she can see into their minds. She feels physically connected, and any threat to them is a threat to her.

We've decided the **main event in the external pressure 1** is:

> **Jaz's actions create a situation where one of her beloved dogs is in danger.**

Now Jaz's life is getting more difficult. She's torn between finding out who killed her husband and keeping herself and her dogs safe. We're bringing her closer to her lowest moment in the story.

We haven't added any characters yet, but we're pretty sure Jaz is going to have a close friend she loses. At this point in the outline, we don't need to know. We do need to know that the action will devastate Jaz.

The first external pressure ends with the reader being unsure if the dog survives.

We decided the main event in the **external pressure 2** is:

> **Jaz saves her dog from death but loses her to dognapping.**

This is similar to Jaz saving a dog in the inciting incident, but this time she didn't save her fully. We like the symmetry here.

She's now under pressure to find out who killed her husband and find her dog. It's time to really increase the obstacles. We know someone close to Jaz will die in plot point 2, so let's force her to make a terrible choice.

We decided the main event in **the external pressure 3** is:

> **Jaz's friend is in danger, and Jaz must decide to go after her friend or her dog.**

We know the main event in **plot point 2** is:

> Jaz's actions cause someone close to her to die.

And now we are onto something. As soon as we reviewed the main event in plot point 2 together with the external pressures, we can see the third external pressure must make Jaz choose between two bad options. Without this process, we might not have found this delicious tidbit.

This is also hinting we need to go back in the outline and add a character. If Jaz is going to lose someone close to her, the relationship between the two characters must be outlined. This character relationship will make up a subplot for the story.

My Fairy Assassin

We need to look at the **reaction to the middle plot point**.

Liv looks for her time lost sister.

Because Liv is distracted by the broken world, Liv looks for her sister in the wrong place. This takes her farther away from reaching her story goal of saving her sister and creates external pressures.

Keeping the environment from being harmed threatens Liv's mission. If she abandons her mission, then she abandons her sister, but she could save the world. Now she has a decision to make. Save her sister or save the world. The reader will hope for both and fear the worst.

We decided the main event in the **external pressure 1** is:

> **Liv finds out her sister and a time lost fairy are being held hostage by the scientist.**

Now Liv's life is getting more difficult, bringing her closer to her lowest moment in the story. Something must go wrong when Liv saves her sister.

We decided the main event in the **external pressure 2** is:

> **Liv saves her sister and the fairy, but part of the fairy wing breaks off during the rescue.**

To keep the emotional roller coaster going, we want Liv to think she's making progress in the next scene.

We decided the main event in the **external pressure 3** is:

> Liv talks to the scientist and believes she's convinced him not to use the fairy wing.

Your Fun Outlining Task

Review the following for your story.

- Skeleton blurb
- Middle plot point
- Reaction to the middle plot point

1. Use these three items to determine the main events in the three external pressure scenes.
2. Add these new scenes to your growing outline.

Where to Next?

Once the reader sees the external pressures the protagonist must face, they'll hope the protagonist will succeed, but they won't be sure. These pressures are pushing the protagonist to their lowest point in the story.

To reach plot point 2, we need a lead-up to plot point 2.

Lead-Up to Plot Point 2

The goal of this scene is to build up to plot point 2 where the protagonist will be at their lowest point in the story. This is the scene where they don't believe they can achieve the story goal. The actions they've taken since the middle plot point have caused them to get farther from the story goal, and they don't understand how to recover.

At this point in the story, they are desperate to achieve their goal and are realizing their actions have caused the disaster they are living.

When outlining this scene, look to see what would make the protagonist realize they really want the story goal for themselves.

Here's what you need to outline this scene.
- Your skeleton blurb.
- The main events for each of the external pressure scenes.
- The main event in plot point 2.

Evolution

First, let's recall the external pressures we just outlined.

External Pressure 1:

Jaz's actions create a situation where one of her beloved dogs is in danger.

External Pressure 2:

Jaz saves her dog from death but loses her to dognapping.

External Pressure 3:

Jaz's friend is in danger, and Jaz must decide to go after her friend or her dog.

The main event in plot point 2 is:

Jaz's actions cause someone close to her to die.

We mentioned in the section on external pressures that we must add a new character. In this scene, we're going to show how close Jaz is to this character. We're also going to show how much Jaz needs this character. We could even foreshadow the trouble coming in plot point 2. We're going to show Jaz having a falling out with this character, so she's alone in her quest to find her husband's killer.

This gives us amazing insight into what we need to add to the Act I outline. We've just shown ourselves one character who must be introduced in Act I is Jaz's friend. When you have moments like these, go to the Act I outline and add the scene. You'll see this in the next section for *Evolution*.

This is an exciting moment, because if we add a scene between the opening image and the inciting incident, we see we've added a scene leading up to the inciting incident that mirrors the scene leading up to plot point 2. This will be exciting for the reader.

The scene we chose to add in Act I is:

Introduce Supporting Character:

Jaz has a friend who she will lose in plot point 2.

Knowing that, we decided the **lead-up to plot point 2** is:

> **Jaz tries to save both her friend and her dog.**

My Fairy Assassin

In the last part of the outline, we focused on the external pressures.

External Pressure 1:

Liv finds out her sister and a time lost fairy are being held hostage by the scientist.

External Pressure 2:

Liv saves her sister and the fairy, but part of the fairy wing breaks off during the rescue.

External Pressure 3:

Liv talks to the scientist and believes she's convinced him not to use the fairy wing.

The main event in Plot Point 2 is:

The time portal fails, and Liv cannot save her sister.

It seems logical that Liv thinks she's solved her story goal of saving the eco-ark and will want to return home. Before she can do that, we're going to cause a serious problem for her.

We decided the **lead-up to plot point 2** is:

> **Liv discovers the scientist is going to make the environmentally disastrous invention from a fairy wing.**

Your Fun Outlining Task

Review the following:
- Your skeleton blurb. Our guess is you have this front and center by now.
- The main event in the three external pressure scenes.
- The main event in plot point 2.

Your fun tasks:
1. Use this information to create the main event for the lead-up to plot point 2.
2. Add the new scene to your outline.

Where to Next?

Soon we'll get to the final act. Every story needs an ending. And our ending is going to relate to the skeleton blurb. Before we go there, take a look at the outline for *Evolution* and *My Fairy Assassin*.

Evolution Act 1 & Act 2 Outline

Act 1

Opening Image:

Jaz abandons her family and bolts from her husband's funeral.

Introduce Supporting Character:

Jaz has a friend who she will lose in plot point 2.

Lead-Up to the Inciting Incident:

Jaz is at home and suicidal.

Inciting Incident:

Jaz saves a dog's life and gains the ability to see into the dog's mind.

Reaction to the Inciting Incident:

Jaz's first dog vision hints at her husband's murder.

Resistance to the Story Goal:

Jaz resists believing her husband was murdered.

Lead-Up to Plot Point 1:

Jaz believes the dog visions are real.

Act 2

Plot Point 1:

Jaz uses a dog vision and finally believes her husband was murdered.

Reaction to Plot Point 1:

Jaz reacts internally to her husband being murdered and searches for clues.

Goal Attempt 1:

Jaz uses a clue found in reaction to plot point 1 and fails. She won't use dog visions in this attempt.

Goal Attempt 2:

With the help of a friend, Jaz uses a dog vision to search for her husband's killer and fails.

Goal Attempt 3:

Jaz reacts to an event and combines traditional investigative methods with dog visions to search for her husband's killer.

Lead-Up to the Middle Plot Point:

Jaz uses a dog vision and finds a clue. She celebrates she can now use the visions to find out who killed her husband.

Middle of Act 2

Middle Plot Point:

Jaz sees a new dog vision. She misinterprets the vision, and it leads her on the wrong path to finding her husband's killer.

Reaction to the Middle Plot Point:

Jaz acts on the misunderstanding in the dog vision.

External Pressure 1:

Jaz's actions create a situation where one of her beloved dogs is in danger.

External Pressure 2:

Jaz saves her dog from death but loses her to dognapping.

External Pressure 3:

Jaz's friend is in danger, and Jaz must decide to go after her friend or her dog.

Lead-Up to Plot Point 2:

Jaz tries to save both her friend and her dog.

My Fairy Assassin Act 1 & Act 2 Outline

Act 1

Opening Image:

Liv's world, the eco-ark, is falling apart.

Lead-Up to the Inciting Incident:

Liv finds out her sister is missing and presumed dead.

Inciting Incident:

Liv discovers her sister is not dead yet but is stuck in a dying fairy world.

Reaction to the Inciting Incident:

Liv enters the fairy world to save her sister.

Resistance to the Story Goal:

Liv resists believing she is capable of changing things.

Lead-Up to Plot Point 1:

Liv starts to see the fairy rules are ones that need following.

Act 2

Plot Point 1:

Liv's sister is dying, and Liv must learn to time travel to save her.

Reaction to Plot Point 1:

Liv must choose a fairy time travel partner, who shows her she must pass three tests in order to time travel.

Goal Attempt 1:

The maze test. This is based on the idea that humans lose all sense of direction, and only if she can get through the maze will she survive.

Goal Attempt 2:

The arrows test. If Liv gets the straightest arrow, she will get the power to choose who she will bond with.

Goal Attempt 3:

The truth test: Liv misunderstands the Salmon of Truth and thinks she's failed the test.

Lead-Up to the Middle Plot Point:

Getting dressed to time travel.

Middle of Act 2

Middle Plot Point:

Liv time travels.

Reaction to the Middle Plot Point:

Liv looks for the time lost sister.

External Pressure 1:

Liv finds out her sister and a time lost fairy are being held hostage by the scientist.

External Pressure 2:

Liv saves her sister and the fairy, but part of the fairy wing breaks off during the rescue.

External Pressure 3:

Liv talks to the scientist and believes she's convinced him not to use the fairy wing.

Lead-Up to Plot Point 2:

Liv discovers the scientist is going to make the environmentally disastrous invention from a fairy wing.

Chapter Nine: Outlining Act 3

We're closing in on the outline. Doesn't that feel great? Can you feel the excitement as your story outline develops?

Act 3 shows the consequences of everything that happened in Act 2 and is where you take your protagonist from their lowest point to the climax scene to the resolution.

You already know the first half of plot point 2 was their lowest point in the story, and the second half of plot point 2 was their decision to go after the story goal like never before.

Act 3 must:

1. Keep the reader reading the novel to the last scene.
2. Answer all the reader's questions about the story world.
3. Answer all the reader's questions about the relationships between the characters.
4. Answer all the reader's questions about the plot.
5. Show the protagonist addressing the story goal in the climax of the book.

But first, the scenes in bold are the new scenes needed in the Act 3 outline.

- Plot Point 2

- **Reaction to Plot Point 2**
- **Lead-Up to the Climax**
- Climax
- **Reaction to the Climax**
- **Resolution**
- **Closing Image**

You can always add to the list. We're giving you a starting point.

Your Fun Outlining Task

1. Add the following five scenes to your outline. Next, you're going to create the main events for each of these scenes.

- Reaction to Plot Point 2
- Lead-Up to the Climax
- Reaction to the Climax
- Resolution
- Closing Image

Where to Next?

You won't be surprised when we say we're going to show you how to outline Act 3.

Reaction to Plot Point 2

The reaction to plot point 2 is the moment the protagonist will learn how to become resilient. Yes, the climax scene is the reason we read. But when a reader reads the reaction to plot point 2, they learn how the protagonist will surmount terrible moments in life.

This scene and the insights the protagonist learns must be well-structured, so the scene won't be forgotten.

Because wow, what a scene. This is one of the scenes in the book showing humanity or lack of humanity depending on your protagonist.

The reaction to the darkest moment in the protagonist's story is what makes the climax believable and inevitable.

This is the phoenix scene of the whole story. Plot point 2 is the place where all hope is lost. This scene comes from the ashes of plot point 2.

Evolution

To find the reaction to plot point 2, we'll use the skeleton blurb and the main event for plot point 2. You can see now why we insisted you write the skeleton blurb before you started to outline your novel.

The Skeleton Blurb for *Evolution* is:

Jaz Cooper must find out who killed her husband using her ability to see into dogs' minds; otherwise, she might die.

The Main Event in Plot Point 2 is:

Jaz's actions cause someone close to her to die.

No one reacts well to losing a friend. This is something everyone can relate to. Whether we lost a friend because of a misunderstanding, because of mixed loyalties, because of death, or for no reason at all, it's happened to us all. That's what makes this a strong plot point 2. It's a universal experience.

We decided we want to give the reader a breather here. Scenes leading up to plot point 2 should be active and full of tension. We haven't written them yet, or even outlined them all, but we know enough to assume the reader needs a breather. This means we're going to add a sequel scene after plot point 2. The scenes leading from plot point 2 to the climax are going to build in tension and speed up in pacing.

So, we're happy with the decision of using a sequel scene to follow plot point 2. You might choose to use an action scene.

We're going to keep Jaz at a low point as she reacts. We're going to give her time to grieve the loss of her friend, but we're not going to let her figure what it means to her. Yet.

Plot point 2 has made it harder for Jaz to reach her story goal. Without her friend, she's lost. She doesn't know how to cope. She must turn back to the dog visions for help.

We decided Jaz's **reaction to plot point 2** is:

> **Grieving, Jaz turns to her dog visions for help.**

My Fairy Assassin

We decided Liv wants the scientist to stand trial for his crimes against nature. We don't know what those crimes are yet. We do know the scientist wanted to destroy the world.

We decided the main event in the **reaction to plot point 2** is:

> **Liv destroys the fairy wing, so the scientist will not be able to use it.**

This trial must be fair. That cannot happen as her fairy accomplice is unable to lie, and Liv must overcome her hatred for the scientist to give him a fair trial; otherwise, the magic might not be enough.

Your Fun Outlining Task

When you know the main event in your plot point 2, think about how the light of hope will get switched back on for the protagonist. What will they find within themselves that will bring about this change? Will they have a realization? Will the internal voice be strong? Will the protagonist go back to a place they emotionally know well, but see it in a new light?

This scene must re-light the hope. And this must come from within the protagonist.

Your fun task:
1. Create the main event in the reaction to plot point 2
2. Add it to your outline.

Where to Next?

Let's get tight with the story goal. You know the story goal from your blurb. This next scene is going to show what it means to the story and the protagonist's journey.

Protagonist Understands the Story Goal

The main event in this scene must build on what the protagonist learned in plot point 2 and the realization that happened in the reaction to plot point 2.

Remember, in plot point 2 the protagonist learns the final piece of information they need to address the story goal, and in this scene, they understand what they learned.

Throughout the story, the protagonist has started to realize that they are missing some of what they need to address the story goal. The protagonist is not conscious of their knowledge gap. If you've set this up well, the reader will understand the knowledge gap and that will cause tension throughout the story.

In Act 3, part of getting the protagonist ready to address the story goal is making this sequel scene about the process the protagonist goes through.

The protagonist must go through ordeals, and those ordeals must have an effect on the protagonist. This sequel scene is about the reader seeing the protagonist process or react to the ordeals that you outlined in the second half of Act 2 in the external pressure scenes.

The understanding of the story goal and the understanding of themselves is a profound moment in the story.

This sequel scene is where the protagonist figures out what the story goal means, and it forces them to make a decision or take a new course of action. This propels them into the next scene.

If you're writing a story where the protagonist doesn't change, this is the point in the story where they act on the final piece of information they learned in plot point 2. They may not change internally, but they do change their external actions in a significant way based on this new information.

The protagonist either changes internally or they change their external actions. In both cases, you'll create a strong story.

Evolution

The main event in this scene is going to relate to Jaz's weakness. We're not exactly sure how Jaz must change because we haven't identified her weakness in the inciting incident yet. It's time to do that.

Some writers know the protagonist's weakness before they start outlining. This is great news if you do. Just remember to put it in the inciting incident scene.

If you notice at this point there is no clear weakness in the inciting incident, then it's time to discover the weakness. The outline you've created so far will help.

The clue for *Evolution* is that Jaz can see into the minds of dogs. This is something that could bring her closer to dogs and distance her from people. She'll be unique in the world and carry this as a secret. And this thought led us to decide Jaz's weakness is she doesn't trust people. We may make this a stronger weakness later. For now, it's enough to get us through the outline.

We decided the main event in the **protagonist understands the story goal** is:

> **Jaz realizes she has isolated herself and can't cope with life alone.**

My Fairy Assassin

Liv understands that for the fair nature of the world to take place, the scientist must get his chance to speak, and he also must get his chance to listen.

Until this point, Liv hasn't understood the world is not always clear cut, and that she must understand there are two sides to every story. That being said, Liv will also learn to trust not only her instincts, but that love can conquer everything. Forgiveness is a superpower, and the key to unlocking anything is love.

We decided the main event in the **protagonist understands the story goal** is:

> **Liv learns there are two sides to every story.**

Your Fun Outlining Task

Go back to the inciting incident and determine what could hint that the protagonist understands the story goal or what hints at a new piece of information that will change the protagonist's external actions. If you can't figure that out yet, put a placeholder scene here and keep going.

Your fun task:
1. Create the main event in the protagonist understands the story goal scene.
2. Add it to your outline.

Where to Next?

We're almost at the climax. Just one more scene to add.

Lead-Up to the Climax

In the climax, the reader will discover if the protagonist achieves the story goal. The lead-up to the climax is used to raise the anticipation the reader feels for the upcoming climax scene.

This scene must not outshine the climax, meaning the main event must not have more tension and conflict than the climax.

All scenes in a book should be there for a reason, and this scene performs a supporting role. It lays the foundation, so the climax scene has a strong base to grow and blossom from.

Evolution

We know the main event in the **climax** scene is:

Using a dog's vision, Jaz discovers who killed her husband.

In the lead-up to the climax, Jaz is going to trust a person instead of a dog vision. This will be a mistake. We need her to trust the dog vision in the climax.

We decided the main event in the **lead-up to the climax** is:

> **Jaz trusts a person over her dog,
> and this causes a disaster.**

In the climax, Jaz discovers who the murderer is. And this comes at a cost.

In the reaction to the climax, Jaz knows she failed at fully trusting people. She's gone back to trusting dogs first. This will keep her from having truly intimate relationships.

My Fairy Assassin

The main event in the **climax** scene is:

> Liv saves her sister by reopening the time portal and injuring the scientist.

The skeleton blurb is:

> Liv Wright must use the fairy time portal to save her fairy assassin sister; otherwise, a scientist will destroy the world.

For Liv to succeed at achieving the story goal written in the skeleton blurb, the main event in the lead-up to the climax must show the power of forgiveness and how that is the most powerful magic in the world.

This is a moment that Liv does not realize will fix the world. Love is good, but forgiveness is the greatest love you can give. It heals everything.

We decided the main event in the lead-up to the climax is:

> **Liv must help grow the fairy wing back, then Liv can open the time portal.**

Your Fun Outlining Task

Refer to:
- Your skeleton blurb.
- The main event for the climax scene.

Your fun task is:
1. Create the main event for the lead-up to the climax scene.
2. Add this to your outline before moving on to the next scene.

Here we get to an interesting place in the outlining process. You started by outlining the five story arc scenes using the skeleton blurb. After you outline the main event in the lead-up to the climax, review the main event in the climax scene. Does it still make sense?

You still don't need to know the "how" of the main event. Check the "what" of the main event.

You've had a lot of creative ideas and made many creative choices by this point in the outlining process. These ideas and choices could have changed how you want to resolve the story goal. If it did, go back and update the main events in the relevant scenes before continuing with the rest of the outline.

Your outline is your guide. If your story changes as you create the outline, or later as you write the scenes, then change the outline. The outline will help you choose what to change and keep the story structurally strong.

Otherwise, keep going.

Where to Next?

It's on to the reaction to the climax. This is a scene readers love. They get to see how the protagonist reacts to the events in the story.

Reaction to the Climax

Readers love reaction scenes. These are scenes where they get to see how the character feels and behaves when something major happens in their life. We all are curious, and we all think we'd behave in a certain way. But you're never sure until an event happens to you.

The story is now over. The reader knows if the protagonist achieved the story goal, so this is the most important reaction scene. After this, we head to the resolution of the story.

The purpose of this scene is let the reader know how the climax affected the protagonist.

Evolution

The Skeleton Blurb is:

Jaz Cooper must find out who killed her husband using her ability to see into dogs' minds; otherwise, she might die.

The main event in the Lead-Up to the Climax is:

Jaz trusts her friend over a dog, and this causes a disaster.

The main event in the Climax scene is:

Using a dog's vision, Jaz discovers who killed her husband.

We have followed Jaz through the outline, and we know Jaz acquired her ability to see into a dog's mind early in the story. We showed her succeeding and failing at using the dog visions.

Because she used the dog visions to finally find her husband's murderer, we decided the main event in the **reaction to the climax** scene is:

Jaz learns she values dogs as much as people.

This is something we can use when we outline the subplots for *Evolution*. By outlining the main plot first, we've discovered Jaz distrusts people. In the next level of outlining, or when we write the draft, this will give us ideas for creating a subplot around Jaz's weakness.

My Fairy Assassin

The Skeleton Blurb is:

Liv Wright must use the fairy time portal to save her fairy assassin sister; otherwise, a scientist will destroy the world.

The main event in the Lead-Up to the Climax is:

Liv must help grow the fairy wing back, then Liv can open the time portal.

The main event in the Climax is:

Liv saves her sister by reopening the time portal and injuring the scientist.

By the time we reached the main event in the reaction to the climax, we saw the image of the ending so clearly that we knew we would have to go back and thread the scientist into the story.

We need an antagonist, and we decided a king must be introduced in Act 1, so his presence and threat to Liv create tension. This is such an exciting development. Our fairy antagonist arrived. Doesn't that show you there is a bit of magic in this process?

When we outline the subplots, the king will join the cast of characters.

We decided the main event in **the reaction to the climax** is:

The world and Liv's sister are no longer dying.

Your Fun Outlining Task

Refer to the following:
- Your skeleton blurb.
- The main event in the lead-up to the climax.
- The main event in the climax.

Your fun task is:
1. Create the main event to the reaction to the climax.
2. Add the scene to your outline.

Where to Next?

We're off to the resolution. This is the scene where you'll ensure your readers leave the novel satisfied.

Resolution

This is where all the loose ends are tidied up. The main event in the reaction to the climax scene showed your reader how the protagonist reacted to the main event in the climax.

The main event in the resolution will show how the protagonist's world changed because of the events in the story.

Evolution

In the main event in the reaction to the climax, Jaz learns she values dogs as much as people.

This scene must show how her ordinary world is different from what it was at the beginning of the story. The story opens at her husband's funeral before she gained the ability to see into a dog's mind. The funeral tells us she was recently widowed. We involved dogs in every story arc scene, and they were crucial to Jaz solving the murder.

As we think through this, we can see in Jaz's ordinary world she was a normal human. Once she gained the ability to see into a dog's mind, this was no longer true. Jaz is going to have an extreme connection with dogs.

We decided the main event in the **Resolution** is:

> **Jaz decides to keep her ability to see into a dog's mind a secret.**

My Fairy Assassin

Again, we have to use what we know so far.

The Skeleton Blurb is:

Liv Wright must use the fairy time portal to save her fairy assassin sister; otherwise, a scientist will destroy the world.

The Main Event in the Climax Scene is:

Liv saves her sister by reopening the time portal and injuring the scientist.

The old future died, but a new future was salvaged.

The Main Event in the Reaction to the Climax is:

Liv is relieved the world and her sister are no longer dying.

We decided the main event in the **resolution** is:

> **Liv accepts the fairy world as part of her world.**

Your Fun Outlining Task

Can you believe you've come this far? You almost have a story outlined.

Refer to the following:
- Your skeleton blurb.
- The main event in the opening image.

- The main event in the lead-up to the climax.
- The main event in the climax.

Your task is to
1. Create the main event for the resolution.
2. Add that scene to your outline.

Where to Next?

One more scene to add, and you're done.
Next, we'll take a look at the closing image. This one will be easy.

Closing Image

You're so close to finishing your story outline! Now it's time for the closing image. This is the last scene your reader experiences before closing your book. Give it emotional sizzle.

You need a scene that mirrors the opening image. This is the final image you'll leave the reader with, and if it mirrors the opening image, the reader will feel a sense of satisfaction. This is where you take the opening image and look at how to mirror what happened. This mirroring shows how the story has affected the protagonist and the characters in the story. In Chapter Four: Skeleton Synopsis Theory, the "What is Mirroring?" section will help guide you.

If you didn't create a main event for the opening image when you started the outline, now is the time to do that. You have enough information, and together with the closing image we hope the opening image becomes clear.

Evolution

For *Evolution*, the **opening image** is

:
Jaz abandons her family and bolts from her husband's funeral.

This gives us a big hint for the closing image. We think Jaz should be somewhere that's happy. Somewhere opposite to a funeral. She runs away from her family in the opening image, so for a mirror we chose to have her go to her husband's grave with her family.

We decided the main event in the **closing image** is:

> **Together with her family, Jaz visits her husband's grave.**

My Fairy Assassin

One of the pleasures of outlining is looking back at the opening image. The opening image shows Liv's world, the eco-ark, is falling apart.

Now, how can we do the exact opposite? Instead of her world falling apart, we decided to show Liv with her family doing something normal.

We decided the main event in the **closing image** is:

> **Liv is getting ready for a family meal out, when her mother and sister come in and give her a gift, tickets to see A Midsummer Night's Dream at the Globe Theater.**

Your Fun Outlining Task

You're at the final fun outlining task for the main plot of your novel.
1. Use the following to decide what the main event in your closing image is:

    a   Skeleton blurb

    b   Opening image

2. Add this final main event to your outline.

Where to Next?

First, it's time to celebrate. You've created an outline that will lead you to a structurally sound novel. That's amazing.

Now it's time to go deeper into your outline.

Huh? You thought we were just creating a story outline. We're going to give you one more gift. One more secret unlocked. A secret that's going to help you speed through your first draft.

When you're ready, continue reading. We are going to show you how to outline a scene, so you can outline structurally sound scenes for every scene in your novel.

Evolution Act 1, Act 2, & Act 3 Outline

Act 1

Opening Image:

Jaz abandons her family and bolts from her husband's funeral.

Introduce Supporting Character:

Jaz has a friend who she will lose in plot point 2.

Lead-Up to the Inciting Incident:

Jaz is at home and suicidal.

Inciting Incident:

Jaz saves a dog's life and gains the ability to see into the dog's mind.

Reaction to the Inciting Incident:

Jaz's first dog vision hints at her husband's murder.

Resistance to the Story Goal:

Jaz resists believing her husband was murdered.

Lead-Up to Plot Point 1:

Jaz believes the dog visions are real.

Act 2

Plot Point 1:

Jaz uses a dog vision and finally believes her husband was murdered.

Reaction to Plot Point 1:

Jaz reacts internally to her husband being murdered and searches for clues.

Goal Attempt 1:

Jaz uses a clue found in reaction to plot point 1 and fails. She won't use dog visions in this attempt.

Goal Attempt 2:

With the help of a friend, Jaz uses a dog vision to search for her husband's killer and fails.

Goal Attempt 3:

Jaz reacts to an event and combines traditional investigative methods with dog visions to search for her husband's killer.

Lead-Up to the Middle Plot Point:

Jaz uses a dog vision and finds a clue. She celebrates she can now use the visions to find out who killed her husband.

Middle of Act 2

Middle Plot Point:

Jaz sees a new dog vision. She misinterprets the vision, and it leads her on the wrong path to finding her husband's killer.

Reaction to the Middle Plot Point:

Jaz acts on the misunderstanding in the dog vision.

External Pressure 1:

Jaz's actions create a situation where one of her beloved dogs is in danger.

External Pressure 2:

Jaz saves her dog from death but loses her to dognapping.

External Pressure 3:

Jaz's friend is in danger, and Jaz must decide to go after her friend or her dog.

Lead-Up to Plot Point 2:

Jaz tries to save both her friend and her dog.

Act 3

Plot Point 2:

Jaz's actions cause someone close to her to die.

Reaction to Plot Point 2:

Grieving, Jaz turns to her dog visions for help.

Protagonist Understands the Story Goal:

Jaz realizes she has isolated herself and can't cope with life alone.

Lead-Up to the Climax:

Jaz trusts a person over her dog, and this causes a disaster.

Climax:

Using a dog's vision, Jaz discovers who killed her husband.

Reaction to the Climax:

Jaz learns she values dogs as much as people.

Resolution:

Jaz decides to keep her ability to see into a dog's mind a secret.

Closing Image:

Together with her family, Jaz visits her husband's grave.

My Fairy Assassin Act 1, Act 2, & Act 3 Outline

Act 1

Opening Image:

Liv's world, the eco-ark, is falling apart.

Lead-Up to the Inciting Incident:

Liv finds out her sister is missing and presumed dead.

Inciting Incident:

Liv discovers her sister is not dead yet but is stuck in a dying fairy world.

Reaction to the Inciting Incident:

Liv enters the fairy world to save her sister.

Resistance to the Story Goal:

Liv resists believing she is capable of changing things.

Lead-Up to Plot Point 1:

Liv starts to see the fairy rules are ones that need following.

Act 2

Plot Point 1:

Liv's sister is dying, and Liv must learn to time travel to save her.

Reaction to Plot Point 1:

Liv must choose a fairy time travel partner, who shows her she must pass three tests in order to time travel.

Goal Attempt 1:

The maze test. This is based on the idea that humans lose all sense of direction, and only if she can get through the maze will she survive.

Goal Attempt 2:

The arrows test. If Liv gets the straightest arrow, she will get the power to choose who she will bond with.

Goal Attempt 3:

The truth test. Liv misunderstands the Salmon of Truth and thinks she's failed the test.

Lead-Up to the Middle Plot Point:

Getting dressed to time travel.

Middle of Act 2

Middle Plot Point:

Liv time travels to save her sister.

Reaction to the Middle Plot Point:

Liv looks for her time lost sister.

External Pressure 1:

Liv finds out her sister and a time lost fairy are being held hostage by the scientist.

External Pressure 2:

Liv saves her sister and the fairy, but part of the fairy wing breaks off during the rescue.

External Pressure 3:

Liv talks to the scientist and believes she's convinced him not to use the fairy wing.

Lead-Up to Plot Point 2:

Liv discovers the scientist is going to make the environmentally disastrous invention from a fairy wing.

Act 3

Plot Point 2:

The time portal fails, and Liv cannot save her sister.

Reaction to Plot Point 2:

Liv destroys the fairy wing, so the scientist will not be able to use it.

Protagonist Understands the Story Goal:

Liv learns there are two sides to every story.

Lead-Up to the Climax:

Liv must help grow the fairy wing back, then Liv can open the time portal.

Climax:

Liv saves her sister by reopening the time portal and injuring the scientist.

Reaction to the Climax:

Liv is relieved the world and her sister are no longer dying.

Resolution:

Liv accepts the fairy world as part of her world.

Closing Image:

Liv is getting ready for a family meal out, when her mother and sister come in and give her a gift, tickets to see *Midsummer Night's Dream* at the Globe Theater.

Chapter Ten: The Full Story Outline

Now that we've outlined the story structure for *Evolution* and for *My Fairy Assassin,* you can see that if we each used this outline to write a draft, each story would still be unique.

We've created an outline that is structurally sound and leaves room for the artist, you the writer, to get creative.

When Are You Done Outlining?

Outlining is a spectrum.

When your fingers are itching to write, that is the best time to get started. If you hit a roadblock when you're writing, come back to your outline for inspiration.

Writing is a passion, and we all want to write well. Outlining can do this for you.

Outlining the story before you write the first draft means the story structure is there. When you edit your story, you will be a very strong position, where the edit will not be about making huge changes, but more about making smaller changes.

The Story Outline

We were tempted to list the outline here and call it the final story outline, but we didn't. This is a process that will evolve all the way until you have an after-draft outline that you create when you start a story edit of your novel. We show you how to create an after-draft outline in *Secrets to Editing Success: The Creative Story Editing Method.*

For now, the story outline is:

- Opening Image
- Lead-Up to the Inciting Incident
- Inciting Incident
- Reaction to the Inciting Incident
- Resistance to the Story Goal
- Lead-Up to Plot Point 1
- Plot Point 1
- Reaction to Plot Point 1
- Goal Attempt 1
- Goal Attempt 2
- Goal Attempt 3
- Lead-Up to the Middle Plot Point
- Middle Plot Point
- Reaction to the Middle Plot Point
- External Pressures 1
- External Pressures 2
- External Pressures 3
- Lead-Up to Plot Point 2
- Plot Point 2
- Reaction to Plot Point 2
- Protagonist Understands the Story Goal
- Lead-Up to the Climax
- Climax
- Reaction to the Climax
- Resolution
- Closing Image

Outlining   Secrets   Unlocked

Chapter Eleven: Outlining a Scene

Now that you've finished outlining your story, it's time to outline a scene. Just like your story structure, every scene in your novel must be structurally sound.

We've included this section to help you outline at the scene level because outlining a scene is the next level of depth in the outlining process.

In this chapter, we'll give you the theory you need to outline a scene successfully. In the next chapter, we're going to show you how to outline the five story arc scenes.

Before we get to that, we'll show you how to create a scene skeleton blurb. We're not referring to the story blurb or the (story) skeleton blurb. We are at the scene level. The scene skeleton blurb will be your North Star for scene outlining.

As you have seen from the story outlining, stories, no matter the genre, have a structure. They have an inciting incident, a plot point 1, a middle plot point, a plot point 2, and a climax.

A scene has a similar structure.

The structure of a scene depends on six story elements. If you need a review of story elements, read *Secrets to Editing Success: The Creative Story Editing Method*.

If you use the story elements we suggest, you'll create structurally strong scene outlines before you write your first draft. Our process encourages creativity and efficiency and is focused on creating scene structures that keep readers engaged.

Here are the story elements needed to structure a scene.
1. Entry Hook
2. POV Goal
3. Scene Middle
4. Scene Climax
5. Exit Hook
6. Scene Name

We'll go into the details of each one of these, but first we'll explore how they work for the reader.

An **entry hook** makes the reader want to read the scene. Entry hooks do this by making the reader ask a question they hope to get answered in the scene or in the following scenes.

The **POV goal** gets the reader into the driver's seat of the scene. The POV character for the scene strives to reach the scene goal, and the reader follows the action this goal brings, or the thought process that the POV character goes through when reacting to the action in a previous scene.

The **scene middle** is when the POV character gets proactive. If done well, this draws the reader farther into the scene. This moment can cause the POV character to pivot, and the reader will be riveted to what made them pivot.

The **scene climax** addresses the POV goal. This means that the reader will know if the POV character was successful or not in achieving the POV goal that was set up at the start of the scene.

Next, we come to the exit hook. **Exit hooks** cause the reader to ask more questions. A question they want answered. Imagine being the reader who has followed the POV character. The scene climax either addressed the POV character's goal, partially addressed it, or didn't address it. Without an exit hook, the reader might put the book down.

The **scene name** should be easy to find from the above story elements. The scene name will be part of your outline and will be tightly linked to the main event you defined for each scene.

Knowing you have these six scene story elements, you can see how you're making your scene outline structurally strong, even before you write the scene.

We're not writing the scene yet, because we want to make sure each scene is structurally strong before we write it. This is what we refer to as creatively efficient.

You've created a story outline, and you'll use that outline to create scene outlines. We'll show you what a scene skeleton blurb is, and you'll write that for every scene before you write the scene.

Then you'll use the six story elements we listed above and get that scene outline written.

Is there a secret to the order that will improve the speed with which you can create the scene outline?

Yes.

Funnily enough, it's like the order we recommended for the story outline.

The secret order for outlining scenes is:

1. List the POV character's goal.
2. List the entry hook.
3. List the scene climax.
4. List the scene middle.
5. List the exit hook.
6. List the scene name.

We're going to show you how to use each of these, so the story elements support the story you want to tell.

When you outline a scene using these story elements, you can gauge if the scene is related to the story goal and whether it has the right energy the scene needs in that part of the story.

Scene outlining is an important skill to have.

When outlining, you'll save loads of time writing a scene. You'll also save time performing a story edit, because both your story outline and scene outlines are structurally sound.

Ours is a process you can replicate for every novel you write.

Caution

> **Not every scene must contain a beginning, a middle, and an end in the final draft.**

You get to decide how you're going to put your scenes into a sequence within the story.

You may decide to have a scene that shows only the beginning and the middle, and the climax for that scene comes later in the story. This sets up an exit hook at the middle of the scene and the reader has to wait for the result. You can use this technique to create suspense in your story.

By outlining your scenes now as if they have a beginning, a middle, and an end, it will be easier to see how you want to structure the final story.

Where to Next?

Let's write scene skeleton blurbs together. After the scene skeleton blurb, we're going to explain the story elements needed to outline a scene. Following the explanations, we'll outline the five story arc scenes.

Scene Skeleton Blurbs

You've written your story skeleton blurb, so you know what it is and how valuable it has been to the story outlining process. Now we're going to show you how to write a scene skeleton blurb. That's a gift we're giving you that will stay with you forever.

We're getting close to the end of our secrets.

Here's the next one we'd like to whisper in your ear.

Chapter Eleven: Outlining A Scene

You can outline every scene using the same method and still write unique scenes.

A scene skeleton blurb is a promise to yourself that you will write each scene using a strong structure. It's a promise that the events in each scene will be related to the story goal and story stakes. These promises are powerful and are only for you. Each scene is a mini-story that must deliver on the promise you outlined.

Imagine outlining and knowing what each scene promises. Imagine having a fast and repeatable method to outline each scene.

We're going to give you that gift, too.

With scene outlining, we're taking the concept of story outlining one step deeper.

We're going to show you how to create a scene skeleton blurb, just like you created a story skeleton blurb.

And we're going to use that blurb to outline scenes.

What Is a Scene Skeleton Blurb?

Here is a reminder of what the **story skeleton blurb** is. The story skeleton blurb has three parts:

- The protagonist
- The story goal
- The story stakes

In sentence form, this is: [The protagonist] must do something [story goal]; otherwise, there will be consequences [story stakes].

Let's build on the story skeleton blurb to create a **scene skeleton blurb**. To do that, we need three story elements:

- The point of view (POV) character (just like we needed the protagonist)
- The POV character's scene goal (just like we needed a story goal)

- The scene stakes (just like we needed the story stakes)

To find the scene stakes, ask what happens if the POV character fails to achieve the scene goal?

There are three simple steps to creating a scene skeleton blurb.

Step 1: Choose the POV Character

The first step in outlining any scene is to choose the POV character for that scene. In stories with multiple point of view characters, the POV character does not have to be the protagonist in every scene.

Choosing the point of view character is an artistic choice.

If you choose a single point of view for the entire novel, you're deciding the reader will only know what that character knows.

If you choose to write your story from multiple points of view, you're deciding the reader will know more than the protagonist knows. This creates knowledge gaps, which in turn creates tension.

It's best to show the reader if the story is a single point of view story or a multiple point of view story before the end of Act 1.

Step 2: Define the POV Character's Scene Goal

Strong scene goals always relate to the main story goal. Scene goals, like story goals, are external and measurable in that the reader can tell if the POV character achieved the goal or not. The goal is what the POV character is trying to achieve in the scene. By the end of the scene, either the POV character achieves the scene goal, they partially achieve it, or they don't. If this doesn't happen, the scene is not strong enough.

> **The scene goal is critical to the success of your scene outline and the success of your novel.**

Step 3: Define the Scene Stakes

The scene stakes are the impact on the POV character, other characters, or the story world if the POV character doesn't achieve the scene goal. The stakes must make the reader worry. The answer to "What if the POV goal fails?" will show you if there are scene stakes.

The Scene Skeleton Blurb

We've included three scene skeleton blurbs here to show what we're striving for before you start outlining a scene.
- The first scene skeleton blurb is for this chapter in *The Secrets to Outlining a Novel*.
- The second is for plot point 1 in *Evolution*.
- The third is for plot point 1 in *My Fairy Assassin*.

We started with plot point 1, because just like it was the first scene we created the main event for, it's the first scene we are going to create a scene outline for.

Secrets to Outlining a Novel

For *Secrets to Outlining a Novel* the Scene Skeleton Blurb is:
- **POV Character:** The writer.
- **Scene Goal:** Understand how to use a scene skeleton blurb.
- **Scene Stakes:** The writer can't outline a structurally sound scene.

In a full sentence, we have:

> **The writer must understand how to use a scene skeleton blurb; otherwise, they can't outline a structurally sound scene.**

Evolution

In *Evolution,* the Story Skeleton Blurb is:

Jaz Cooper must find out who killed her husband using her ability to see into dogs' minds; otherwise, she might die.

We're going to write the scene skeleton blurb for plot point 1.

The Main Event in Plot Point 1 is:

Jaz uses a dog vision and finally believes her husband was murdered.

We know the **POV character** in plot point 1 is Jaz because she's the protagonist, and plot point 1 is a story arc scene. The POV character for all the story arc scenes must be the protagonist.

We also know the Main Event for Lead-Up to Plot Point 1:

Jaz believes the dog visions are real.

This gives us so many ideas for a scene goal. We decided that in the opening part of the scene, Jaz needs to interact with a dog as she's reacting to the events of the previous scene where she received proof the dog visions are real. She sees a vision where her husband is frantically searching for something in his office.

That's a big event to come to terms with.

The POV Goal Becomes:

Search her husband's home office.

We're already thinking of the middle of the scene where Jaz discovers a clue. And the climax where the dog shows Jaz the clue means her husband was murdered.

Now all we have left is the stakes.

What if Jaz fails to achieve her goal? In this case, if Jaz doesn't search her husband's office, she won't find the clue, and she won't see the vision that confirms her husband was murdered. If she doesn't learn her husband was murdered, she won't know her life is in danger.

The **stakes** are Jaz won't understand her life is in danger. But most importantly, if Jaz doesn't find the clue confirming her husband was murdered, she won't accept the story goal. This means there is no story.

The scene skeleton blurb becomes:

POV Character:

Jaz Cooper.

POV Scene Goal:

Organize her husband's home office.

Scene Stakes:

Jaz won't understand her life is in danger, and she won't accept the story goal.

Written as a sentence, the Scene Skeleton Blurb becomes:

> **Jaz must organize her husband's office; otherwise, she won't learn her life is in danger, and she won't accept the story goal.**

My Fairy Assassin

In *My Fairy Assassin*, the Story Skeleton Blurb is:

Liv Wright must use the fairy time portal to save her fairy assassin sister; otherwise, a scientist will destroy the world.

We're going to write the scene skeleton blurb for plot point 1.

The main event in plot point 1:

Liv's sister is dying, and Liv must learn to time travel to save her.

Remember, we know the **POV character** in plot point 1 is Liv because she's the protagonist, and plot point 1 is a story arc scene. The POV character for all the story arc scenes must be the protagonist.

We Also Know the Main Event for Lead-Up to Plot Point 1:

Liv starts to see the fairy rules are ones that need following.

From these main events, we have many ideas for a scene goal. We decided that in the opening part of the scene, Liv has seen how violent the fairies are when their rules are not followed. So, in this scene, Liv must learn how she can volunteer to save her sister and not fall foul of the fairies. The POV goal is to volunteer to time travel.

Liv saw one of the fairies getting murdered for not following the fairy protocol.

That's a big event to come to terms with.

The POV goal becomes:

Volunteer safely to time travel.

The reader and the protagonist will be aware that if Liv does not volunteer in a safe way, then she will be killed, so the tension is built in from the previous scene. Then there will be how this is done. This should be the mid-point of the scene, where Liv steps forward.

Now, all we have to do is focus on the stakes.

What if Liv fails to achieve her goal? If Liv doesn't volunteer in the correct way, not only will her sister die, but she will too.

The **stakes** are Liv and her sister will both die.

The scene skeleton blurb becomes:

POV Character:

Liv Wright.

POV Scene Goal:

Volunteer safely to time travel.

Scene Stakes:

Liv and her sister will both die.

Written as a sentence, the Scene Skeleton Blurb becomes:

> **Liv Wright must volunteer safely to time travel; otherwise, Liv and her sister will both die.**

This outline scene blurb is the promise that is in the scene. When you come to write the scene, this will help with the drafting.

Your Fun Outlining Task

This is the first scene you're going to outline, and you'll need the scene skeleton blurb to outline the scene.
Your fun task is:
1. Create a scene skeleton blurb for plot point 1 of your story.

You'll create the scene skeleton blurb for the remaining story arc scenes right before you outline those scenes.

Where to Next?

You've already followed this process to outline your story.
Let's discover more about how the story elements are going to change the way you outline forever.
We're going deeper now and are going to show you how to outline a scene. We'll start with the story elements you need, and then we'll outline all five story arc scenes. After that, you'll be an expert at scene outlining and can apply that process to every scene in your story.

By the time you're finished, you'll have a strong story outline and a strong scene outline for every scene in the story. How cool is that?

You'll outline these scenes in this order first:
1. Plot point 1
2. Inciting incident
3. Plot point 2
4. Climax
5. Middle plot point

Just like a specific order helped you create a story outline, a specific order will help create scene outlines. These five scenes are the spine of your story. You may find when you outline the scenes that you have to return to your story outline and update it. That's OK because it means the process is working.

Let's look at the story elements you need.

Chapter Twelve: Six Story Elements You Can't Live Without

Meet the Story Element: Point of View Character's Goal

Every scene will have a point of view character. That character's goal for the scene will drive the action for the scene.

The POV character's goal is what the POV character wants to achieve in the scene. This element drives the scene, and everything in the scene relates to the POV character striving for the goal. At the climax of the scene, the POV character either achieves, partially achieves, or doesn't achieve the goal.

To create tension in every scene, make the reader wait until the scene climax before addressing the POV character's goal, or leave it open and use it as an exit hook.

The POV character's goal is external and makes the POV character move. The character is chasing after something or someone they want. So, by using this story element in your outline, you'll make sure the character is in motion. This is important because a character in motion increases the story's pacing.

If the scene is a sequel scene, where the POV character is reacting to the previous scene, then the character's goal is still external. Don't confuse a sequel scene with a scene that doesn't have action. The purpose of a sequel scene is to show how the main event in the previous scene impacts the POV character. The scene shows the character reacting to the event while they are pursuing an external scene goal.

Where Do You Place the POV Character's Goal?

The reader should understand the POV character's goal in the first paragraph or two of every scene. Otherwise, the scene opening will drag. This is a similar problem to the inciting incident occurring too late in the story, making the story drag.

Where to Next?

Now you know what a POV character's goal is, so we can move on to the scene entry hook.

Meet the Story Element: Scene Entry Hook

An entry hook draws the reader into the scene. It leaves readers with questions they must have answers to. It makes the reader want to keep reading.

You must answer the questions created by the entry hook at some point in the story. They don't have to be answered in this scene. A reader might put the book down if they get answers too quickly. So, think about the questions you are raising and also the placement of the answers.

You must make the reader ask, "What's going to happen next?"

Perhaps an entry hook is like poetry: You can hint at something without starting it outright. Let's look at a wonderful example from Jenna Moreci's book *The Savior's Champion*.

The first word in the book is one of the best entry hooks around. Here it is:

Run.

Isn't that a powerful entry hook? Look at what it makes us ask.

In the novel, the word run is in italics, so it's an internal thought. Who is thinking this? What are they running from? Where are they that they must run? Why are they running? How will they get away?

All from one word. And we must read on.

Where Do You Place the Entry Hook?

An entry hook should be in the first sentence or paragraph of every scene.

Where to Next?

Your scene outline has an external POV character's goal and an entry hook that forces the reader to ask questions, so now it's time to move on to the scene climax. Yes, you read that correctly. We are outlining a scene in a nonlinear fashion, just like we outlined the story in a nonlinear fashion.

Meet the Story Element: Scene Climax

Let's take a moment to recap. You've stated a scene POV character's goal. The climax of the scene is going to address the goal in some form. This makes it easy to know what the scene climax is about.

There are three obvious ways to address a POV character's goal. The POV character is successful, partially successful, or unsuccessful. This seems obvious, but it's easy to create a scene climax that is not related to the scene goal. If this happens, the story won't flow.

If the POV character changed their scene goal at the middle point of the scene, then the climax can address either goal. It's up to you as the artist to decide whether the climax will address the original or the updated scene goal.

Scenes get interesting when you address the POV character's goal in a way the reader is not expecting.

When readers say a scene was inevitable but had a twist, it means you built this into the deep structure of the scene.

Where Do You Place the Scene Climax?

The scene climax should come near the end of the scene. Once the POV character's goal is addressed, the scene is over. Did you notice the scene climax comes near the end but not at the end? That's because an exit hook is either part of the climax or it comes after the climax.

Where to Next?

So far, you have the POV character's goal, the entry hook, and the scene climax. There are two more parts to the scene we need to outline before you can name the scene and add a scene name to your story outline.

We have enough information to state what happens in the middle of the scene, so let's get the scene middle outlined.

Meet the Story Element: Scene Middle

The scene middle is the moment in the scene where the POV character becomes proactive instead of reactive. This proactivity is caused by a mid-scene event.

What happens in the first half of the scene creates a sense of proactivity in the POV character at the scene middle.

The scene middle must not be ignored when it comes to outlining a scene. The creativity that comes from outlining your POV character's goal and the scene climax creates the perfect springboard for outlining the middle.

So far, we know the POV character's goal, the entry hook, and the scene climax.

Like a novel, the scene middle is a turning point in the scene. Give your POV character a new problem to face.

At the middle of a scene, events will either get worse or better for the POV character. The POV character should be driving the action forward until the climax of the scene.

The character's proactivity can come from conflict in the first half of the scene, a revelation, an object being found, or a myriad of other ways.

Where Do You Place the Scene Middle?

We know this is obvious, but we're going to state this, anyway. The scene middle occurs somewhere around the middle of the scene.

Where to Next?

It's time for the exit hook. This is the question you leave with the reader, so they must read the next scene.

Meet the Story Element: Exit Hook

An exit hook drives your reader to read the next scene. An exit hook will stop the reader from putting the book down, which means it's critical for writing a tension-filled story.

Like an entry hook, the exit hook is about the questions the reader asks themselves. The exit hook is the connection from one scene ending to the next scene starting.

If you think like a reader, the end of the scene is the perfect place to put down a book, so the energy the question creates must be enough to get the reader to read one more scene.

What question do you want to leave the reader with when they end the scene? The questions don't have to be answered in the next scene, but they must be answered by the end of the story. Unanswered questions are called loose ends, and readers don't like them.

Where Do You Place the Exit Hook?

The story element is different from the others when it comes to where to place the exit hook. Usually, the exit hook is the last event that happens in a scene. It's either part of the scene climax or occurs after the scene climax. Note that an exit hook can be placed anywhere in a scene. If the question the reader is left with by the end of the scene is strong enough to keep the reader engaged, it can come earlier in the scene. An entry and exit hook can even be the same sentence. Sometimes an entry hook is so strong, it can carry the reader through multiple scenes.

Where to Next?

Finally, we get to naming the scene. Scene naming is gold. It's a powerful tool that will get you from outlining to a finished story. We don't see how anyone can outline, write, or edit a draft without naming every scene.

Meet the Story Element: Scene Name

The scene name is your private name for the scene. It's what you call the scene, so you know what the scene is about. You don't need to include the scene name in your story.

Scene names show you the scene is focused. Once you've written your draft, if you can name every scene in three words or fewer, you have a focused scene.

During the outlining phase, you can use more than three words. You'll use the scene names to write your story. You'll use the scene names when you edit your draft. Scene names are important to the outlining, writing, and editing process.

You can choose the POV character's goal or the scene climax as the name. Both are important to the outline. As long as the name shows you what the scene is about, it will help you write the scene.

Where Do You Place the Scene Name?

This is a trick question. The scene name is for your use only. We're not suggesting you add a name to each scene in your novel. We're suggesting you name each scene, so you can reference the scene easily.

At the outlining phase, be as concise as possible. It must be enough information for you to know what the scene is about.

Where to Next?

It's time to dive deep into the five story arc scenes.

Without a bit of story knowledge, outlining these scenes can seem unfathomable. And yet, once you know the secrets to their outlining, you will get the thrill that comes from outlining these five story arc scenes.

Chapter Thirteen: Outlining the Five Story Arc Scenes

You've already outlined your novel. That's amazing. You can start writing, or you can do a bit more outlining.

One route forward is to outline the structure of the five story arc scenes. We like this option because it helps get a powerful grasp on the structure of a scene and of the story. It's great practice, and if you can write a scene with the structure of a scene in mind, you'll have a stronger first draft to edit.

The events that take place in the inciting incident can take place in one scene or over several scenes. The same is true for plot point 1, the middle plot point, plot point 2, and the climax.

For outlining purposes, we'll treat each story arc scene as one scene. You can create multiple scenes after you've finished your outline and you're adding depth to each story arc scene.

Remember we created the main events for the story arc scenes in a nonlinear order? That was:

1. Plot point 1
2. Inciting incident
3. Plot point 2
4. Climax
5. Middle plot point

To outline the five story arc scenes, we're going to use the following six story elements in the following nonlinear order.

1. POV goal
2. Entry hook
3. Scene climax
4. Scene middle
5. Exit hook
6. Scene name

If you're excited to write, try drafting one of the scenes. Then come back and continue outlining. The goal is to motivate you. You know yourself best, and sometimes a scene screams to be written.

In your scene outline, the protagonist must be the point of view character for the inciting incident, plot point 1, the middle plot point, plot point 2, and the climax. This is non-negotiable for the outline. This will focus your story on one character and make it easier to outline. You'll get to add more characters later.

Your Fun Outlining Task

To break this into manageable parts, we'll give you a fun task for each of the story arc scenes in the following sections.

Where to Next?

The first scene we outline is plot point 1.
Why?
Because this is the most important scene in an outline. It's the scene the story hinges on. After that, we'll have enough information

to outline the inciting incident. Yes, you guessed it. We're outlining in a nonlinear fashion again.

Outlining Plot Point 1

We've already created the main event in the lead-up to plot point 1, plot point 1, and the reaction to plot point 1. This gives us the main events in the scene before and the scene after plot point 1.

These three scenes will help you determine the POV character's goal for plot point 1. We're going to show you how. Then you'll apply that technique as you add more scenes to your outline.

We're going to use these scenes along with the story blurb and scene skeleton blurb to outline plot point 1 for *Evolution* and *My Fairy Assassin*.

We're moving from outlining the story structure to outlining a scene. Before we do that, let's recall what a plot point scene must accomplish.

It must:
1. Contain new information about the story goal.
2. Change the story direction.
3. Raise the stakes.
4. Be full of tension.
5. Be written in the protagonist's POV.

This tells us we'll have to pull out the story skeleton blurb again.

Evolution

The story blurb is:

Jaz Cooper must find out who killed her husband using her ability to see into dogs' minds otherwise, she might die.

Lead-Up to Plot Point 1:

Jaz believes the dog visions are real.

Plot Point 1:

Jaz uses a dog vision and finally believes her husband was murdered.

Reaction to Plot Point 1:

Jaz reacts internally to her husband being murdered and searches for clues.

As we recommended, we've listed the main event in the lead-up to plot point 1, plot point 1, and the reaction to plot point 1.

In Chapter Eleven: Outlining a Scene, we wrote the scene skeleton blurb for plot point 1.

> **Jaz must organize her husband's office; otherwise, she won't learn her life is in danger, and she won't accept the story goal.**

This shows us Jaz is the POV character, she has a goal, and the stakes are high.

That's not enough for us to have a full scene. The outline needs to link back to the main story goal.

So far, we know we want dogs and the dog visions to play a big role. The story goal is to use those visions to find out who killed Jaz's husband.

Plot point 1 must be about the visions, so Jaz needs a dog with her. We've just added a character to the scene. The dog is our new character.

For *Evolution*, we decided:

POV Goal:

Search her husband's home office.

Entry Hook:

A dog vision shows Jaz a scene where Jaz's husband is searching frantically for something in his office. The hook is: what was he searching for?

Scene Climax:

Dog vision shows her husband's murder. She believes this because the previous scene proved to her the visions show actual events.

Scene Middle:

Dog vision hints her husband was in trouble. Jaz pushes for more.

Exit Hook:

How will Jaz react to seeing her husband's murder? The exit hook must be about the murder, as solving the murder is the main story goal.

Scene Name:

Jaz's husband murdered. By outlining this story element last, it's easy to see from the scene middle and scene climax what the scene name should be.

At this stage, you don't need to know everything. This is enough for us to know the scene relates to the main story goal, has an event forcing Jaz to go after the story goal, and creates high stakes.

> **Remember, you're creating an outline of the scene and not a draft, so keep the word count low.**

My Fairy Assassin

The Story Blurb is:

Liv Wright must use the fairy time portal to save her fairy assassin sister; otherwise, a scientist will destroy the world.

We have three scenes.

Lead-Up to Plot Point 1:

Liv starts to see the fairy rules are ones that need following.

Plot Point 1:

Liv's sister is dying, Liv must time travel to save her sister.

Reaction to Plot Point 1:

Liv commits to passing the time travel test.

The Scene Skeleton Blurb:

Liv must get permission to time travel; otherwise, her sister dies.

Let's think about the lead-up to plot point 1. This scene will cause the decision to time travel and save the sister. The sister is not lost in time. It's the sister's time traveling partner who is lost in time. The sister is travelsick from not being reunited with her travel partner. So, Liv must discover the sister is on death's door.

So now she has decided to save her sister, she must find out how to go about that.

The temptation is to put in too much here. Remember to keep going back to the POV goal.

What will the POV character do in the following scene that increases the tension from the previous scene?

Next, Liv must find out how she will qualify to become a time-traveling sister savior.

POV Goal:

Be accepted as a fairy time traveler.

Entry Hook:

Liv sees an entity trying to steal her sister's soul.

Scene Climax:

The leader of the fairies decrees that Liv must pass the fairy tests to decide her own partner.

Scene Middle:

Liv discovers why she needs to be Fairy ready.

Exit Hook:

If Liv does not pass, she might not be able to save her sister.

Scene Name:

Permission Requested.

Your Fun Outlining Task

Read the scene skeleton blurb that you wrote for your plot point 1 scene. in Chapter Eleven: Outlining a Scene.

Go back to your outline and review:
- The Story Blurb
- Lead-Up to Plot Point 1
- Plot Point 1
- Reaction to Plot Point 1

Using this information, outline the following story elements in the following order:
1. POV Goal
2. Entry Hook
3. Scene Climax
4. Scene Middle
5. Exit Hook
6. Scene Name

The scene name is extremely important. At the end of the outlining process, the scene names will show you your full story outline. When you draft the story, you may change the names. When you perform a story edit, you may change them again. This list is your live story structure.

You may find the story elements come to you in a different order than what we've listed above. That's great. Do these in the fastest way you can. We're not dictating the order. We're giving you our process. Our gift is you can adapt that to a process that works for you.

Where to Next?

And there you have one scene outlined. Keep in mind when you write the scene, you may come up with other ideas for the events in the scene. For now, keep going with the remaining story arc scenes.

Outlining the Inciting Incident

Before we outline the inciting incident, let's recap what the inciting incident must do. It must:
1. Cause the protagonist to react to the action stated in the scene's main event. The reaction is the start of the protagonist's journey.
2. Be early in the story.
3. Relate to the story goal stated in the story skeleton blurb.
4. Be told from the protagonist's point of view.

Without an inciting incident, the protagonist's life goes on as usual, and there is no story. The inciting incident must be connected to the story skeleton blurb and to plot point 1.

The main event in the inciting incident hints at the story goal that's in your story skeleton blurb.

We just created the scene outline for plot point 1, and we can use that.

Before we can outline the inciting incident, we must create a scene skeleton blurb for the scene. The scene skeleton blurb is created from these three story elements:

1. The point of view (POV) character
2. The POV character's goal
3. The stakes for the POV character (What if the goal fails?)

We'll need the main event for the following scenes to help us create the scene outline.

1. Lead-up to the inciting incident
2. Inciting incident
3. Reaction to the inciting incident

Evolution

The Story Skeleton Blurb is:

Jaz Cooper must find out who killed her husband using her ability to see into dogs' minds; otherwise, she might die.

Let's create the scene skeleton blurb by following the process we described in Chapter Eleven: Outlining a Scene.

The three main events we need are:

1. Lead-Up to the Inciting Incident: Jaz is at home feeling suicidal.
2. Inciting Incident: Jaz saves a dog's life and gains the ability to see into its mind.
3. Reaction to the Inciting Incident: Jaz's first vision hints at murder.

In the lead-up to the inciting incident, Jaz is feeling suicidal. Something happens in that scene to make her want to live. We don't know what yet, and that's OK.

The POV character's goal in the inciting incident must fit what the lead-up to the inciting incident shows, and it must lead to the reaction to the inciting incident.

We decided to put a dog in distress and make Jaz's goal to be: Save the dog.

This has obvious stakes. The dog's life.

Something must happen to give Jaz the ability to see into a dog's mind. The goal and the stakes relate nicely to the story blurb.

The POV Character:

Jaz Cooper.

The POV Goal:

Save the dog.

The Stakes (What If the Goal Fails):

The dog's life.

The Scene Skeleton Blurb is:

Jaz must save the dog; otherwise, the dog will die.

Now, we get to look at:

- Entry Hook
- Scene Climax
- Scene Middle
- Exit Hook
- Scene Name

The entry hook must be strong enough to pull Jaz from her suicidal thoughts in the lead-up to the inciting incident. It must also make the reader ask a question.

We decided for the **entry hook**, Jaz will hear a dog in distress. She's a dog person and can't ignore the call.

Since this is the hook and the POV goal, the **climax** is going to be Jaz rescuing the dog. The dog is going to be a major character in the book, so Jaz must save her.

The **scene middle** is when the POV character gets proactive. Jaz is going to put her life in danger to save the dog. We know the main event in the scene is the dog infecting Jaz. For Jaz to get infected by the dog, the dog must break Jaz's skin and contaminate her with saliva. We'll make this the scene middle.

Exit hooks cause the reader to ask more questions. In the next scene we've called "reaction to the inciting incident," Jaz gets a vision that hints at her husband being murdered. So, in this scene, we decided the exit hook is: Jaz sees into the dog's mind but thinks she is in shock and doesn't believe the vision. The exit hook is: Are the visions real?

This gives us a scene outline for the inciting incident.

Entry Hook:

Distress call by dog.

POV Goal:

Save the dog.

Scene Middle:

The dog breaks Jaz's skin and contaminates Jaz.

Scene Climax:

Jaz rescues the dog.

Exit Hook:

Is Jaz's dog vision real?

Scene Name:

Jaz saves dog.

Again, you see how easy it is to name a scene when you've outlined it first. Just wait till you name all scenes. It's going to be a structurally sound outline. Let's test the inciting incident against plot point 1.

For plot point 1, the main event is:

Jaz believes the dog visions are real.

The scene outline is:

Entry Hook:

What was her husband searching for in the dog vision?

POV Goal:

Organize her husband's home office.

Scene Middle:

Dog vision hints her husband was in trouble. Jaz pushes for more.

Scene Climax:

Dog vision shows her husband's murder. She believes this because the previous scene showed her the visions show actual events.

Exit Hook:

How will Jaz react to seeing her husband's murder?

Scene Name:

Jaz's husband murdered.

The inciting incident hints at the dog visions. Plot point 1 uses the visions to confirm Jaz's husband was murdered. The outline of scenes between the inciting incident and plot point 1 now has a path.

From the inciting incident to the lead-up to plot point 1, we'll go on a journey of building up the dog visions until Jaz believes they are true.

My Fairy Assassin

The Story Skeleton Blurb is:

Liv must use a fairy time portal to save her sister; otherwise, a scientist will destroy the world

Again, we are going to create the scene skeleton blurb by following the process we described in Chapter Eleven: Outlining a Scene.

The three main events we need are:
1. Lead-up to the Inciting Incident: Liv finds out her sister is missing and presumed dead.
2. Inciting Incident: Liv discovers her sister is not dead yet but stuck in a dying fairy world.
3. Reaction to the Inciting Incident: Liv enters the fairy realm to save her sister.

In the lead-up to the inciting incident, Liv finds out her sister is missing and presumed dead. Liv is now broken.

Remember, the POV character's goal in the inciting incident must fit what the lead-up to the inciting incident shows, and it must lead to the reaction to the inciting incident.

We decided to show that the sister was stuck in the fairy world, and she was in danger. This means Liv will attempt to enter the fairy world to save her sister.

This has obvious stakes. It is not easy to enter the fairy world. If someone enters the wrong portal, they die. This entrance test is related to saving the sister, and it also has an inherent risk.

The POV Character:

Liv Wright

The POV Goal:

Enter the Fairy World

The Stakes:

Liv and her sister's lives

The Scene Skeleton Blurb is:

Liv must use a fairy time portal to save her sister; otherwise, a scientist will destroy the world.

In addition to the POV goal, we get to look at:
- Entry Hook
- Scene Climax
- Scene Middle
- Exit Hook
- Scene Name

We decided that for the entry hook, Liv sees her sister in a bay leaf. She asks the fairy how this is possible. The fairy says she has a choice to make. She can go into the fairy world, or she can wait. Liv says she wants to enter the fairy world even though it's dangerous.

The entry hook and the POV goal show us that the **scene climax** is Liv going through the fairy door into the fairy world.

The **scene middle** is when the POV character gets proactive. Liv sees her sister in distress in the bay leaf.

Exit hooks cause the reader to ask more questions. In the next scene we've called "reaction to the inciting incident," Liv finds herself in the fairy realm. So, in this scene, we decided the exit hook is: has Liv chosen the right door to live? The exit hook is: Does Liv make it?

This gives us a scene outline for the inciting incident.

Entry Hook:

Liv sees her sister laughing in a bay leaf.

POV Goal:

Get into the fairy world.

Scene Middle:

Liv sees her sister in distress in the bay leaf.

Scene Climax:

Liv goes through the fairy door into the fairy world.

Exit Hook:

Does Liv make it?

Scene Name:

Liv's fairy world entrance

Again, you see how easy it is to name a scene when you've outlined it first. Just wait till you name all scenes. It's going to be a structurally sound outline. Let's test the inciting incident against plot point 1.

The outline of plot point 1 outline is:

Entry Hook:

Liv sees someone trying to steal her sister's soul.

POV Goal:

Be accepted as a fairy time traveler.

Scene Climax:

The leader of the fairies decrees Liv must pass the fairy tests to decide her own partner.

Scene Middle:

Liv discovers why she needs to be Fairy ready.

Exit Hook:

If Liv does not pass, she might not be able to save her sister.

Scene Name:

Permission Requested.

The inciting incident hints of trouble in the fairy world. Plot point 1 confirms the fairy world has rules that need to be obeyed; otherwise, people and fairies die. The outline of scenes between the inciting incident and plot point 1 now has a path.

We'll go on a journey where Liv must learn that not all rules can be broken, but when she's going to break a rule, she must do so for the best reason.

Your Fun Outlining Task

Review the main events for the following scenes:
1. Lead-up to the inciting incident
2. Inciting incident
3. Reaction to the inciting incident

Next, work through the process as we did for *Evolution* and *My Fairy Assassin* and outline your inciting incident.

Where to Next?

We'll keep building the outline in our nonlinear fashion. This means we're going to build the outline for plot point 2 next. We're going to bring Jaz and Liv to their knees. This will be the lowest point for both protagonists in their respective stories.

Outlining Plot Point 2

Let's add the outline for point 2 to our story arc scene outlines. Here's a short recap of what plot point 2 must accomplish.

> **The main event in the plot point 2 scene causes the protagonist to be at their lowest point in the story. Disaster has struck, and they believe they won't achieve their story goal. The reader will worry, too.**

Plot Point 2 must:
1. Be told from the protagonist's point of view.
2. Be written in active form.
3. Cause the protagonist to experience their lowest emotional point of the story so far.
4. Share the final piece of information the protagonist needs to address the story goal.
5. Create a sense of urgency.
6. Mirror plot point 1.

We're going to create a scene skeleton blurb for plot point 2.
- The point of view (POV) character
- The POV character's goal
- The stakes for the POV character (What if the goal fails?)

We'll need the main event for each of these scenes:
1. Lead-up to plot point 2
2. Plot point 2
3. Reaction to plot point 2

Once we have the skeleton blurb, will use our story elements to outline the scene.

Evolution

Let's keep going with our outline of *Evolution*.

Lead-Up to Plot Point 2:

Jaz and her friend discover a devastating clue to husband's past. Jaz and her friend are at odds with what this clue means and how Jaz should act on it.

Plot Point 2:

Jaz's actions cause someone close to her to die.

Reaction to Plot Point 2:

Jaz grieves the loss of a friend and turns to her dog's visions for help.

In the lead-up to plot point 2, Jaz and her friend have a falling out and Jaz needs her back. Her goal for the scene is exactly that. Get her friend back. The stakes are Jaz has to cope with finding her husband's murderer alone.

The Skeleton Blurb for Plot Point 2 becomes:

Jaz must get her friend back; otherwise, she must cope with finding her husband's murderer alone.
Here is the scene outline:

POV Goal:

Get her friend back.

Entry Hook:

Will Jaz's friend forgive her?

Scene Climax:

Jaz's friend dies.

Scene Middle:

Jaz has a dog vision showing her she's right and her friend is wrong.

Exit Hook:

Will Jaz survive alone?

Scene Name:

Jaz alone.

Overview of Scene Outline So Far

And now our outline is gaining momentum. Let's look at the scene outlines together.

Main Event in the Inciting ncident

Jaz saves a dog's life and gains the ability to see into the dog's mind.

For the inciting incident, the scene outline is:

POV Goal:

Save the dog.

Entry Hook:

Distress call by dog.

Scene Middle:

The dog breaks Jaz's skin and contaminates her.

Scene Climax:

Jaz rescues the dog.

Exit Hook:

Is Jaz's dog vision real?

Scene Name:

Jaz saves dog.

Main Event in Plot Point 1:

Jaz uses a dog vision and finally believes her husband was murdered.

For plot point 1, the scene outline is:

POV Goal:

Search her husband's home office.

Entry Hook:

What was her husband searching for in the dog vision?

Scene Middle:

Dog vision hints her husband was in trouble. Jaz pushes for more.

Scene Climax:

Dog vision shows her husband's murder. She believes this because the previous scene showed her the visions show actual events.

Exit Hook:

How will Jaz react to seeing her husband's murder?

Scene Name:

Jaz's husband murdered.

Main Event in Plot Point 2:

Jaz loses friend.

The outline for plot point 2 is:

POV Goal:

Get her friend back.

Entry Hook:

Will Jaz's friend forgive her?

Scene Middle:

Jaz has a dog vision showing her she's right and her friend is wrong.

Scene Climax:

Jaz's friend dies.

Exit Hook:

Will Jaz survive alone?

Scene Name:

Jaz alone.

The story outline is growing. But do the scenes fit together?

The inciting incident hints at the dog visions. Plot point 1 confirms they are real. Plot point 2 uses a dog vision to cause a disaster for Jaz. So far, we're confident our decisions are going to create a story readers love.

My Fairy Assassin

Let's keep going with our outline of *My Fairy Assassin*.

Lead-Up to Plot Point 2:

Liv discovers the scientist is going to make the environmentally disastrous invention from a fairy wing.

Plot Point 2:

The time portal fails, and Liv cannot save her sister.

Reaction to Plot Point 2:

Liv destroys the fairy wing so the scientist will not be able to use it.

The Skeleton Blurb for Plot Point 2 Becomes:

Liv must get through the time portal in time; otherwise, she is stuck in the past.

POV Goal:

Get through the portal.

Entry Hook:

Will Liv get there in time?

Scene Climax:

The time portal is broken.

Scene Middle:

The sister is very close to dying.

Exit Hook:

How can Liv get back to her time with her sister?

Scene Name:

Time portal breaks.

And now our *My Fairy Assassin* outline is gaining momentum. Let's look at the scene outlines together.

Main Event in the Inciting Incident:

Liv discovers her sister is not dead yet but is stuck in a dying fairy world.

For the inciting incident, the scene outline is:

POV Goal:

Get into the Fairy world.

Entry Hook:

Liv sees her sister in a bay leaf.

Scene Middle:

Liv sees her sister in distress in the bay leaf.

Scene Climax:

Liv going through the fairy door into the fairy world.

Exit Hook:

Does Liv make it?

Scene Name:

Liv's fairyland entrance

For plot point 1, the scene outline is:

POV Goal:

Be accepted as a fairy time traveler.

Entry Hook:

Liv sees an entity trying to steal her sister's soul.

Scene Climax:

The leader of the fairies decrees that Liv must pass the fairy tests to decide her own partner.

Scene Middle:

Liv discovers why she needs to be Fairy ready.

Exit Hook:

If Liv does not pass, she might not be able to save her sister.

Scene Name:

Permission Requested.

The Main Event in Plot Point 2:

The time portal fails, and Liv cannot save her sister.

The outline for plot point 2 is:

POV Goal:

Get through the portal.

Entry Hook:

Will Liv get there in time?

Scene Climax:

The time portal is broken.

Scene Middle:

Liv's sister is very close to dying.

Exit Hook:

How can Liv get back to her time and her sister?

Scene Name:

Time portal breaks.

The story outline is growing. But do the scenes fit together?

The inciting incident shows the danger that the sister is in. Plot point 1 confirms Liv's sister is about to die. In plot point 2, when the time portal shuts, the fate of Liv's sister is sealed. So far, we're confident our decisions are going to create a story readers love.

Your Fun Outlining Task

Refer to the main events in these scenes:
- Lead-up plot point 2
- Plot point 2
- Reaction to plot point 2

Your fun tasks are:
1. Create your scene skeleton blurb.
2. Create your scene outline for plot point 2.
3. Put it together with the inciting incident and plot point 1.
4. Check that plot point 1 and plot point 2 mirror each other.

Where to Next?

It's time for the tensest scene in our story. We're going to outline the climax, and it's going to be a whopper.

Outlining the Climax

We're getting excited about our outline. Hopefully, you are, too. We're starting to see our story appear. And now we get to work on the climax. That's always fun.

The rule for the climax, and yes, we said rule, is that the main event in the climax must show if the protagonist achieves the main story goal or not. This is nonnegotiable. If this isn't shown, the scene isn't a climax scene, and the story isn't over.

If there isn't a climax scene that addresses the story goal, there is no story, yet.

Now that we've gotten the rule out of the way, there are other considerations for the climax scene.

To be structurally sound, the climax should:
1. Be told from the protagonist's point of view.
2. Show the protagonist leading the charge to reach the story goal.
3. Be written in active form.
4. Mirror the inciting incident.

Yes, we got a little bossy with that advice. And yes, we feel good about that. A great climax scene will lead to rave reviews. A weak climax scene will leave the reader feeling let down. And a reader who is let down won't recommend your book.

First, we're going to create a skeleton blurb for the climax. This includes:
- The point of view (POV) character
- The POV character's goal
- The stakes for the POV character (What if the goal fails?)

We'll need the main event for each of these scenes to help us create the climax scene outline:
1. Lead-up to the climax
2. The climax
3. Reaction to the climax

Once we have the skeleton blurb, will use our six story elements to outline the scene.

Evolution

The three main events we need to outline *Evolution* are:

Lead-Up to the Climax:

Jaz trusts a person over her dog, and this causes a disaster.

Climax:

Using a dog's vision, Jaz discovers who killed her husband.

Reaction to the Climax:

Jaz learns she values dogs as much as people.

In the lead-up to the climax scene, Jaz trusts the wrong character. This causes a huge problem for her. We don't know what that problem is yet, but as we get deeper into outlining our scenes, we'll figure it out.

This means Jaz's goal in the climax scene is to solve her husband's murder.

Here's something amazing.

> The story skeleton blurb and the scene skeleton blurb become the same for the climax scene and the story. This means we've addressed the story goal.

The Story Skeleton Blurb and the Scene Skeleton Blurb are:

Jaz Cooper must find out who killed her husband using her ability to see into dogs' minds; otherwise, she might die.

We know the structure is strong because the two skeleton blurbs are the same. So, let's outline the climax scene.

The lead-up to the scene causes Jaz to abandon her friend. She's already lost one friend (death at plot point 2), and she's not about to risk another.

POV Goal:

Solve her husband's murder.

Entry Hook:

Jaz faces her husband's murderer alone. Will she survive?

Scene Climax:

With the help of her dog, Jaz captures the murderer.

Scene Middle:

Using a dog vision, Jaz gains an advantage over the murderer.

Exit Hook:

How will Jaz cope with knowledge of who killed her husband?

Scene Name:

Jaz's husband's killer identified.

In the inciting incident, Jaz saves the dog. In the climax the dog helps save Jaz. Here we see how the climax mirrors the inciting incident.

My Fairy Assassin

As we did for *Evolution*, we'll refer to the main events in the lead-up to the climax, the climax, and the reaction to the climax.

Lead-Up to the Climax:

Liv must help grow the Fairy wing back, then Liv can open the time portal.

Climax:

Liv saves her sister by reopening the time portal and injuring the scientist.

Reaction to the Climax:

Liv is relieved the world and her sister are no longer dying.

This means her scene goal is to re-open the time portal, so she can travel through and save her sister.

The scene skeleton blurb and the story skeleton blurb are:

> **Liv must use a fairy time portal to save her sister; otherwise, a scientist will destroy the world.**

Remember, we know the story structure is strong because the two skeleton blurbs are the same.

So, let's outline the climax scene.

The lead-up to the scene gives Liv the enlightenment she needs, and she understands how she can use the magic to reverse the broken portal.

The outline for the climax scene becomes:

POV Goal:

Re-open the time portal.

Entry Hook:

Is getting the fairy wing back enough?

Scene Climax:

Liv travels through the time portal.

Scene Middle:

Liv gets the fairy wing back and injures the scientist.

Exit Hook:

Where will they end up?

Scene Name:

Time portal re-opened.

Your Fun Outlining Task

Review the main event for the following scenes:
- Lead-up to the climax
- Climax scene
- Reaction to the climax

Your fun task is:
1. Create your scene skeleton blurb and scene outline for the climax.
2. Check that the climax answers, either positively or negatively, the story goal.
3. Check that the scene blurb is identical or almost identical to the story skeleton blurb.

Where to Next?

We are nearly at the end of outlining the story arc scenes. We just have the glorious middle scene to outline next. And then we hope you'll be out dancing, singing, or celebrating in the way you celebrate best.

Outlining a Scene Middle

Finally, we land in the middle plot point.

Here's our recap of what a middle plot point should accomplish:

1. Have the main event collide with the protagonist's worldview.
2. Push the protagonist to be proactive instead of reactive.
3. Foreshadow the main event in the climax scene.

There are some great hints above that will help us outline the middle plot point.

Before beginning, review the following:

- Your story skeleton blurb.
- The climax scene skeleton blurb (remember, this should be the same as the story skeleton blurb).
- The main event in the climax scene.
- The main event in the opening image.
- The main event for the middle plot point.
- The main event in the lead-up to the middle plot point.
- The main event in the reaction to the middle plot point.

Evolution

Having specific information to work from helps us determine the outline for the middle plot point. This plot point is often one of the hardest to write, so we'll take any assistance we can.

For *Evolution*, we have:

Climax and Story Skeleton Blurb:

Jaz Cooper must find out who killed her husband using her ability to see into dogs' minds; otherwise, she might die.

Climax Main Event:

Using a dog's vision, Jaz discovers who killed her husband.

Opening Image Main Event:

Jaz abandons her family and bolts from her husband's funeral.

Lead-Up to the Middle Plot Point Main Event:

Jaz uses a dog vision and finds a clue. She celebrates she can now use the visions to find out who killed her husband.

Middle Plot Point Main Event:

Jaz sees a new dog vision. She misinterprets the vision, and it leads her on the wrong path to finding her husband's killer.

Reaction to the Middle Plot Point Main Event:

Jaz acts on the misunderstanding in the dog vision.

Let's get working on our scene outline.

We know the main event in the lead-up to the middle plot point, and this shows us what the goal must be.

POV Goal:

Use dog vision to find more clues.

We know this scene must make Jaz collide with her worldview, so we give it an entry hook related to that.

Entry Hook:

Force Jaz to do something she's uncomfortable with.

This scene climax is related to the story blurb.

Scene Climax:

Dog vision shows the wrong killer.

We'll use the scene middle to show Jaz moving from reactive to proactive. She decides how to act. We'll also use it to mirror the opening image where Jaz reacts badly to her husband's funeral.

Scene Middle:

Jaz faces that her husband is dead and deals with his personal items. She finds new information here.

The next two are easy because we've led ourselves here.

Exit Hook:

How will Jaz act on the new information?

Scene Name:

Jaz on wrong path.

We're done with outlining the story arc scenes for *Evolution* and are confident we can write a first draft from this.

My Fairy Assassin

Remember, having the specific information to work from helps us determine the outline for the middle plot point. This plot point no longer needs to be one of the hardest to write.

For *My Fairy Assassin*, we have:

Climax Scene and Story Skeleton Blurb:

Liv must use a fairy time portal to save her sister; otherwise, a scientist will destroy the world.

Climax Main Event:

Liv reopens the time portal and saves her sister and the world.

Opening Image Main Event:

Liv's world, the eco-ark, is falling apart.

Lead-Up to Middle Plot Point Main Event:

Getting dressed to time travel.

Middle Plot Point Main Event:

Liv time travels.

Reaction to the Middle Plot Point Main Event:

Liv looks for the time lost sister.

Let's get working on our scene outline.

We know the main event in the lead-up to the middle plot point, and this shows us what the goal must be.

In the fairy world, there is a saying: Clothes maketh the fairy. This is true for the fairy and anyone that is associated with the fairy. Fairies take sartorial choices very seriously. Fairies expend a lot of their magic on making their clothes, and anyone who is associated with them looks better. Time travel is a drain on their fairy magic. So, dressing for the time travel means that the magical energy that a fairy would normally expend on the clothing glamour can be redirected to opening up of the time portal.

In wearing fairy's clothes, Liv is wearing color for the first time in her life. Although she is not vain, she feels the clothes are lovely, and yet they are a complete waste of resources. The waste on creating colorful clothing annoys her. The reader will be full of anticipation as the anger that Liv feels, and the importance of the ceremony, means that performing magic is going to be even tougher.

This is an exciting moment. This scene outline has more details than previous scenes. And this is outlining gold. The farther you get into your creative outlining, the more ideas that will spark for you. When you have creative inspirations, add it to your outline.

POV Goal:

Unlock the time travel portal.

We know that this scene must make Liv collide with her world view, so we give it an entry hook related to that.

Entry Hook:

How will Liv perform magic for the first time?

This scene climax is related to the story blurb.

Scene Climax:

Liv walks into the time portal.

We'll use the scene middle to show Liv moving from reactive to proactive. She decides who she will be. We'll also use it to mirror the opening image where Liv's world is falling apart.

Scene Middle:

Liv changes her mind and chooses another fairy to time travel with her.

The next two are so easy to outline they write themselves.

Exit Hook:

Will Liv get through the time travel portal safely?

Scene Name:

Liv opens portal.

We're done with outlining the story arc scenes for *My Fairy Assassin* and are confident we can write a first draft from this.

Your Fun Outlining Task

Review the main events in the following scenes:
- Opening image
- Lead-up to the middle plot point
- Middle plot point
- Reaction to the middle plot point
- Climax

Your fun task is:
1. Create your scene skeleton blurb for the middle plot point scene.
2. Use this information to create your scene outline for the middle plot point scene.

Where to Next?

We're going to bring this all together and help you choose the type of protagonist you need.

Outlining   Secrets   Unlocked

Chapter Fourteen: Bringing It All Together

You've created an outline for the key scenes in your novel. You've outlined the five story arc scenes. This has given you ideas for the remaining scenes.

We started with the five story arc scenes because if one of these scenes is missing, there is no story.

Remember from Chapter Four: Skeleton Synopsis Theory:

Skeleton Synopsis = Skeleton Blurb + 5 Story Arc Scenes + Resolution

The inciting incident shakes up the protagonist's ordinary life.

> **If there is no inciting incident,**
> **there is no story**
> **because all we're reading about is a protagonist's**
> **ordinary life.**

Plot point 1 shows the protagonist accepting the story goal.

> **If there is no plot point 1,**
> **meaning the protagonist doesn't accept the story goal,**
> **then there is no story**
> **because the protagonist doesn't do anything.**

The middle plot point shows the protagonist changing from reactive to proactive.

> **If there is no middle plot point,**
> **the protagonist doesn't drive the story forward and cause problems,**
> **and there is no story.**

Plot point 2 shows the protagonist at the lowest point in the story and gives the protagonist the final piece of information they need to address the story goal.

> **Without the new information learned in plot point 2,**
> **the protagonist cannot address the story goal.**
> **If they can never address the story goal,**
> **the story never ends.**
> **There is no story if there is no plot point 2.**

The climax scene shows whether the protagonist achieves the external story goal, or they don't.

> **If there is no climax scene where the protagonist addresses the story goal, there is no story because the story isn't over.**

The main purpose of the resolution is to give the reader closure after the climax scene. The reader will want to know what the protagonist's world looks like after they have addressed the story goal in the climax.

> **If there is no resolution, the story may have ended**
> **but the reader will not feel satisfied.**
> **You'll still have a story,**
> **only the reader might not read your next book.**

By starting your outline with the five story arc scenes and a resolution, you're guaranteed to create a strong story.

The five story arc scenes give you the spine of your story, and every other scene works to support that story.

You still have choices. After all, this is your story, your outline, and your process. You can either keep outlining or start writing your draft. Either way, you're starting your draft using a structurally sound outline.

Maybe you're closer to the discovery writer end of the writing spectrum and you want to write now. This is a great time to do this. The outline you created has set boundaries for you. If you stay within those boundaries, your artistry will explode. Working within boundaries means you will write a better story. And that's what this process is all about.

We're not done yet. It's time to bring the characters on stage.

Your Fun Outlining Task

This is a big one, so take some time to think about it.
1. Review your story skeleton blurb. Does it need updating based on what you outlined?

Now is the time to do that before we move on to the next step.

Where to Next?

The protagonist.

We promised earlier in this book that creating an outline would help you define who your protagonist is and what type of protagonist they are. And here we go...

What Type of Protagonist Should You Have?

You already know we think of a protagonist as an entity.

There are three types of entities.
1. A single protagonist.
2. A combined protagonist.
3. A group protagonist.

Once you've created your story outline, you'll be able to see what type of protagonist entity suits your story.

The story goal decides whether you have a single protagonist, a dual protagonist, or a group protagonist. It is as simple as that.

If the story goal for two lead characters is not the same, like in some romance stories, then look for the character who has the most to lose and who addresses the story goal in the climax. That is the protagonist.

The Oscars give us a good example of character roles. They give an award for the lead role, and they give an award for the best supporting actor. This is because the supporting character has such a big role, but it doesn't mean they are also a protagonist.

Let's get back to looking at if you want a single, combined, or group protagonist.

Single protagonists are the most common. This is one character's struggle to achieve a story goal.

If two protagonists are fighting for the same goal, they are a combined protagonist. The movie *Thelma and Louise*, written by Callie Khouri, is a great example of a dual protagonist.

Here's our attempt at a skeleton blurb for *Thelma and Louise*.

> **Two women must outrun the cops; otherwise, they will die.**

By the end of an outline, the stakes are clear because the climax scene defines this. The protagonist entity in *Thelma and Louise* is a combined protagonist because there are two characters with the same story goal who are on the same adventure.

A group protagonist can be a small group of sleuths, or it can be a society versus a great threat. Quest stories often fall into this category. *Game of Thrones* is a great example.

We wrote a skeleton blurb for *Game of Thrones: Song of Ice and Fire* by George R.R. Martin.

> **Humans must defeat the White Walkers; otherwise, civilization will end.**

The protagonist entity is the humans. From this, we know we're going to have a group of people who are important to the story, and it will probably be written from multiple points of view.

In a group protagonist story, the stakes always put the whole group at risk. The group has the same story goal, but each character experiences a different adventure.

Your Fun Outlining Task

It's time to figure out who your protagonist is and what type of protagonist entity they are.

To find your protagonist, review your skeleton blurb.

For the protagonist listed in the skeleton blurb, it's time to get specific. You will be able to tell if the protagonist is a single, combined, or group protagonist just by how you named the entity. Did you name the entity by a protagonist's name? Then it's a single protagonist. Did you name it using two names? Then it's a combined protagonist. Did you name it using a group of characters? Then it's a group protagonist.

Is there one character in the skeleton blurb?

Yes?

If you can, name the character. If you can't name the character, that's still OK. As you write your story, you'll figure this out. It's not needed during outlining.

Are there two characters in the skeleton blurb?

Yes?

Then, you at least need to refer to them as Character A and Character B as you write your first draft. You'll be making point of view decisions, and you'll need to decide who is the point of view character for each scene.

Is there a group listed in the skeleton blurb?

Yes?

Chapter Fourteen: Bringing It All Together

Here, you're going to need a list of characters. When you're writing your draft, you can list them as Character A, Character B, Character C, Character D, Character E, and Character F. Six characters are enough to start. You can also name these characters by function.

Your Fun Task

1. Determine the type of protagonist entity that best suits your story.
2. Go back to your outline and add that character(s) to each scene.
3. If there is more than one character in the entity, choose a point of view character for each scene. Don't get stuck here. You can change this later.

Where to Next?

That's up to you. You've finished the first pass of your outline. You may choose to outline at the scene level for every scene you've listed in the story outline.

You may choose to write your story. As you write, keep this outline updated. It's the fastest way to see how the changes you make while writing the story impact the story structure.

In this book, we outlined a linear novel. For those of you interested in more complex structures, read on.

Chapter Fifteen: Outlining Nonlinear Structures

We've outlined a single story arc for a linear plot. As promised in the opening of this book, we're going to give you the process to outline a nonlinear plot.

We're entering advanced outlining techniques here, and we're going to show you how to use the story outline you created while reading this book to create an outline for a story that follows a nonlinear structure.

A linear plot line is a story told in the order it occurs. A nonlinear story is told with flashbacks. Note that a nonlinear story is not a time travel story.

You might want to use a nonlinear structure if you have a large cast of characters, or you have two story lines.

We're going to unlock one more secret here.

You can use the story arc to help you outline a nonlinear story, so the resulting story is structurally sound.

We all know a story has a beginning, a middle, and an end. The beginning must always appear at the beginning, no matter how the story is told. The middle must occur in the middle, and the end must occur at the end. This is true for all stories because a reader experiences a story from the beginning to the middle to the end.

We also know every story includes the five story arc scenes. These are the inciting incident, plot point 1, the middle plot point, plot point 2, and the climax.

Here's where it gets exciting. You can change the order in which the story arc scenes appear in the story, and this is where the story arc is going to help you make sure the story is structurally sound.

The story arc scenes sit on top of the acts and are more flexible in their placement than the acts.

Nonlinear Structures

Nonlinear structures are a huge topic on their own. To keep things simple, we're going to limit the types of structures we cover in this chapter.

We consider the following the main types of nonlinear structures.
1. **Plot point flashback:** This occurs when you open the story with a look at the future (some call this a preview flashback). This is when a novel starts in the future and comes back to the present. This is usually done to hook the reader when the writer needs time to build the ordinary world before the inciting incident occurs.
2. **Bookending the main story arc:** A novel starts in the future, comes back to the present (one long flashback), and ends in the future. There are no flashback scenes between the book-

end scenes.
3. **Dual narrative stories:** There are two story arcs in one story, and one is told in the present, the other in the past. One story will be a flashback. The other won't.

Before getting into the more complicated structures, you might want to re-read the section on protagonists in Chapter Fourteen: Bringing it All Together.

If you don't have a clear protagonist strategy and don't use the story arc to help you outline a nonlinear story, there is a structural risk. The story might not have focus. It might not be clear who the protagonist is or what their story goal is.

Before we move on, let's cover a bit of theory on flashbacks.

> **Flashbacks are a structural choice you make after you've created an outline. We need flashbacks to tell a story in a nonlinear way.**

The movie, *The English Patient*, based on the book written by Michael Ondaatje, when watched from start to finish, has a beginning, a middle, and an end. It's told in the present and in the past. The movie opens with the climax scene of the past and then uses flashbacks throughout the story. Both the past and present story lines follow their own story arc.

A high word count flashback is usually used to show something in the protagonist's past they need to fix.

A short word count flashback is something that occurs closer to the present and is tightly related to what happens after a story arc scene.

Let's set out some guidelines for flashbacks.

1. They are never used to show something that has already been told or shown in the present.
2. They need to be balanced throughout a story. If one suspect in a murder mystery gets a flashback scene, the other suspects must get one, too. If one love interest in a romance gets a flashback scene, the other love interest must get one, too. You

see the idea.
3. If a flashback can be told using description in the present, the event is probably not flashback worthy.
4. A flashback must always be related to the main story goal in the skeleton blurb.
5. A long flashback will affect the structure and must be evaluated in the context of the story arc.

Where to Next?

It's time to make the complicated simple. We'll start with what we call a plot point flashback.

Plot Point Flashback

Let's start with the easier type of nonlinear story. You only need to add one scene to your story outline you created while reading this book, and you've got a plot point flashback outline.

A plot point flashback means opening the novel with a scene that occurs later in the story. It won't be the full scene because it can't be a spoiler. It must hint at something bad without showing if that bad thing happens or not.

A plot point flashback is sometimes confused with a prologue. It is entirely different.

We're going to show you how to outline a plot point flashback. There are some simple structural guidelines to make this work.

You must have a story outline, or you can't know what the plot point flashback will be. Which you do because you just read this book and created a story outline.

Once you choose this structure, there shouldn't be any other flashbacks in the story.

The plot point flashback scene will be part of one of the five story arc scenes that you've already outlined. This must be the case because it has to be a strong hook. You're about to ask the reader to start the story over in the next chapter, so you must motivate them to keep reading.

We already know the five story arc scenes are the key turning points in a story.

Don't choose the inciting incident as the plot point flashback scene. It's too close to the beginning of the story, so it won't work structurally. The hook is not big enough.

If you have a long and slow-paced first act, you could choose plot point one. To make this choice, something bad must happen to the protagonist early in the plot point 1 scene before they decide to accept the story goal.

This means the first act is a flashback starting right after the plot point flashback and ending at plot point 1. After that, the story moves forward in a linear fashion. This is the hardest scene to choose because the stakes are not extreme yet.

The next choice is the middle plot point. This is harder than choosing plot point 2 or the climax. The middle plot point can work because the protagonist experiences a life-changing event that causes them to move from reactive to proactive. Usually, the first half of the middle plot point will be the life-changing event. The reader won't know what it means for the protagonist, so it makes a good hook.

Plot point 2 is an even stronger choice. You can show the protagonist at their lowest point in the story without showing what happens.

The climax works just as well as plot point 2. Only part of the climax can be shown in the plot point flashback if it's going to create a strong hook.

Many books about this type of flashback often state that the scene must be related to the story goal. You've already accomplished that because you outlined each story arc scene and made sure the scenes are related to the story goal you wrote in your skeleton blurb.

Why Use a Plot Point Flashback?

When you look at your outline, is the inciting incident quite late in the appropriate range?

Yes?

Consider a plot point flashback if your inciting incident happens after fifteen percent into the story.

Does your story require a lot of world-building or significant time to set up the ordinary world?

Yes?

Then consider a plot point flashback.

Your Fun Outlining Task

If you've decided to use a plot point flashback:
1. Select the story arc scene that gives the strongest hook. This is most likely plot point 2 or the climax.
2. Add the plot point flashback as the first scene in the story outline.
3. Put the first half of the chosen scene in the new first scene.
4. End that scene on a strong hook.
5. Make sure there are no other flashbacks in the story.
6. Make sure the scene does not give away too much. This means no spoilers.

Where to Next?

We'll move on to the next level of difficulty. We're going to show you how to outline a story with bookended scenes.

Bookending the Main Story Arc

This type of story opens in the present, tells the rest of the story in a long flashback to the past, and ends in the present.

For a plot point flashback, we added one scene to the beginning of the outline you created while reading this book.

For a bookending story, we're going to add two scenes to the outline. You've already outlined the story arc without bookend scenes. Now you get to add two new scenes.

This type of story works well when the novel opens with the protagonist in the present. Something significant will force them to recall the past, and the story will move into a flashback that lasts until the final bookend scene.

The final scene will have a surprise that changes the meaning of the story. This is a must; otherwise, there isn't a reason to bookend the story.

If you choose this technique, every scene between the bookend scenes is told in a linear fashion. Jumping back and forth in time won't work for this structure.

The Titanic, the movie written by James Cameron, is a good example of a bookended story.

Your Fun Outlining Task

If you've decided to use a bookended structure, you have a bit more work to do.
1. Add a new first scene to the outline. End this scene on a strong hook.
2. Add a new final scene to the outline. This is the last scene your reader will read. This scene must answer the hook in the first scene, or this structure won't work.
3. Outline both scenes in the same way we showed you how to outline a story arc scene in Chapter Thirteen: Outlining the Five Story Arc Scenes.
4. Make sure there are no other flashbacks in the story.
5. Check the story arc is still balanced correctly with the new scenes. The Inciting incident could be moved too far into the story, or the climax could be moved too early. You can push the ranges here, but you must still respect the story structure.

Where to Next?

Again, we'll move on to the next level of difficulty. We're going to show you how to outline a dual narrative story.

Dual Narrative Stories

This is one of the more difficult of the nonlinear story types to outline and write. It's almost impossible to write if you haven't created a story outline first. In fact, you'll create two outlines. One for the story told in the past, and one for the story told in the present.

The subject of outlining a dual narrative is a book in itself as there is a spectrum of narrative possibilities.

We'll focus on the most common type of dual narrative story where part of a story is told in the past and part is told in the present.

Outlining Guidelines

1. The opening scene(s) must trigger both story lines.
2. The story is going to alternate between the present and the past.
3. Both stories have the same protagonist.
4. Both stories include the five story arc scenes. Each story has an inciting incident, plot point 1, middle plot point, plot point 2 and a climax.
5. Both stories are told in chronological order.
6. Usually, the story told in the past is the longer story.
7. The two stories are linked. The story told in the present must solve a mystery from the story told in the past.
8. An event in the story told in the past must cause the inciting incident in the story told in the present. This is what links the two stories; otherwise, these are two separate stories, and they don't belong in the same book.
9. The story starts in the past because either plot point 2 or the climax of the story told in the past will trigger the inciting incident for the story told in the present.

We're going to show how to outline a dual narrative novel that will keep the reader engaged. You can probably see that hooks will be a main driver. In our outline below, we chose plot point 2 of the story told in the past to be the inciting incident of the present. You can create this outline using the climax of the story told in the past instead of plot point 2 if that works better for your story.

You've already created a single outline. If you want to use this structure, the easiest way forward is to create a second outline that you're going to weave into the first outline. To move forward, we suggest reading the remaining part of this chapter and then going back and outlining the second story. After that, it's time to combine the two stories into one outline.

How to Outline a Dual Narrative Story

You will create two skeleton blurbs. One for the story told in the past and one for the story told in the present.

You will create two outlines. One for the story told in the past, and one for the story told in the present. You'll follow the same process we showed in this book.

Once the outlines are done, at least done enough, you're going to combine them in a structurally sound way. As before, you can always change the outline as you discover more about the story.

Once there is a story outline for the story told in the past and the story told in present, you'll interweave them. It will be no surprise that you'll use the five story arc scenes as the places in the novel to jump between the past and the present.

Just as a reminder. Here is the story outline for a linear model.

Act 1

Opening Image

Introduce Supporting Character

Lead-Up to the Inciting Incident

Inciting Incident

Reaction to the Inciting Incident

Resistance to the Story Goal

Lead-Up to Plot Point 1

Act 2

   Plot Point 1

   Reaction to Plot Point 1

   Goal Attempt 1

   Goal Attempt 2

   Goal Attempt 3

   Lead-Up to the Middle Plot Point

Middle of Act 2

   Middle Plot Point

   Reaction to the Middle Plot Point

   External Pressure 1

   External Pressure 2

   External Pressure 3

   Lead-Up to Plot Point 2

Act 3

   Plot Point 2

   Reaction to Plot Point 2

   Protagonist Understands the Story Goal

Lead-Up to the Climax

Climax

Reaction to Climax

Resolution

Closing Image

We start our outline for the dual narrative story with the inciting incident from the story told in the present. Plot point 2 is the lowest point for the protagonist in the story told in the past, and this is what triggers the inciting incident in the present.

Plot point 2 is a strong scene that hooks the reader and draws them into Act 3. In a dual narrative story, we're going to use it to jump to the inciting incident in the present.

Here is what the outline looks like.

Present Inciting Incident

The present inciting incident must also serve as the opening image in the story, as that is what the reader experiences first.

The following scenes take place in the present and come after the present-time inciting incident.

- **Present Inciting Incident**
- Present Reaction to the Inciting Incident
- Present Resistance to the Story Goal
- Present Lead-Up to Plot Point 1
- Present Plot Point 1

The first flashback is to the inciting incident in the past. This is the incident that starts the overall story. We stay in the past until the past plot point 1, so we've included those outline scenes here.

Past Inciting Incident (Flashback)

The following scenes take place in the past and come after the past-time inciting incident.

- **Past Inciting Incident**
- Past Reaction to the Inciting Incident
- Past Resistance to the Story Goal
- Past Lead-Up to Plot Point 1
- Past Plot Point 1

Now we've left the reader with a strong hook, and the story will jump back to the present.

Present Reaction to the Present Plot Point 1

We start with the reaction to the present plot point 1, as the reader has already read the present plot point 1 right before we jumped to the first flashback. The following scenes take place in the present and come after the reaction to present plot point 1.

- **Present Reaction to the Present Plot Point 1**
- Present Goal Attempt 1
- Present Goal Attempt 2
- Present Goal Attempt 3
- Present Middle Plot Point

Past Reaction to the Past Plot Point 1 (Flashback)

Now we jump to the past again. The reader has just experienced the present middle plot point. And before that the past point 1. This means it's the perfect place to place the past reaction to the past plot point 1.

The following scenes take place in the past and come after the past reaction to the past plot point 1.

- **Past Reaction to the Past Plot Point 1**
- Past Goal Attempt 1
- Past Goal Attempt 2
- Past Goal Attempt 3
- Past Middle Plot Point

Present Reaction to the Present Middle Plot Point

Because we just placed the past middle plot point, we have another spot to jump to the present. The following scenes take place in the present and come after the present reaction to the middle plot point.

- **Present Reaction to the Middle Plot Point**
- Present External Pressure on Protagonist
- Present Lead-Up to Plot Point 2
- Present Plot Point 2

Past Reaction to the Past Middle Plot Point (Flashback)

The following scenes take place in the past and come after the past-time middle plot point.

- **Past Reaction to the Past Middle Plot Point**
- Past External Pressure 1
- Past External Pressure 2
- Past External Pressure 3
- Past Lead-up to Plot Point 2
- Past Plot Point 2

Present Reaction to the Present Plot Point 2

Because we used plot point 2 as our trigger for the inciting incident in both stories, this is the last time we can use a flashback. The story moves forward in a linear fashion from here to the closing image. The following scenes take place in the present and come after the present-time plot point 2.

- **Present Reaction to the Present Plot Point 2**
- Present Protagonist Understands the Story Goal
- Present Overcome Weakness in the Inciting Incident
- Present Lead-Up to the Climax
- Present Climax
- Present Resolution
- Present Closing Image.

We've seen the climax to both stories, so now the story only moves forward. There are no more

A dual narrative story uses advanced story telling techniques. We've just touched on it here in case you're at this level and it's the type of story you're writing.

Where to Next?

We're going to take a quick look at adding subplots to your outline.

Outlining   Secrets   Unlocked

Chapter Sixteen: Outlining Subplots

You've created a structured outline for your main plot. This means you've got the action of a story outlined.

We haven't dealt with subplots because subplots are easier to outline after the main plot line is outlined first. To keep this book focused on creating a structured main plot, we haven't included a detailed section on subplots.

The plot is the action of the story. The subplots will contain the characters' growth and relationships. Most importantly, you'll show what's at stake for the protagonist via the subplots. The final key scene in a character growth subplot is a scene in Act 3 where the protagonist realizes they must change.

The protagonist figures out what their weakness is and they change who they are fundamentally. This scene is a sequel scene. And then the climax scene will be an action scene where the protagonist shows this change of character in action.

A great subplot won't work until there is a structured main plot. The outline you've just created gives you what you need to add in subplots.

The story goal in the skeleton blurb drives the action in the story. It's what holds the subplots together. Stories without a strong plot line often appear episodic. A series of unrelated subplots can cause this problem.

Subplots must be structured, too.

> **Every subplot must have a beginning, a middle, and an end.**

Every subplot must follow its own story arc with the five story arc scenes. A subplot without structure will be problematic. A subplot that is not connected to the main plot will be problematic.

If you want to add subplots to your outline, go back to the beginning of the book and follow the fun outlining tasks.

Here's a tip to help you.

> **When inserting subplot scenes, position them right before or right after the five story arc scenes of the main plot line.**

These new scenes can be used to support the story arc scenes. They can support changes in the story direction.

The main character of the subplot will be trying to achieve something. Ensure they do this near the climax scene of the main plot. This can happen before, after, or during the climax scene. If the reader doesn't learn whether the subplot goal is achieved, they will be unsatisfied with the story's ending.

A subplot is where the reader understands the stakes for the characters. Understanding what's at stake means the readers will connect even more with the characters. For a subplot to be strong, it will most likely run through two acts of the story. Subplots don't have to start in Act 1, but they can. Starting a subplot in Act 3 is too late to use the subplot to connect readers with the characters but might be okay if you're writing a series and it's a lead-up to the next story.

Here's a second tip to help you.

> **Use your skeleton blurb to check if the subplot is related to the main plot.**

A subplot should start after the main story has started. If the book opens with a subplot, the reader will think they are reading the main plot. This can cause confusion as to what the story is, who the protagonist is, and what the story goal is. All bad things if you want readers to love your story.

Your Fun Outlining Task

1. Create a subplot from scratch.
2. First create a subplot skeleton blurb.
3. Then create a subplot skeleton synopsis.
4. Figure out how many scenes the subplot needs.
5. Choose where each of the subplot plot points should enter the story.
6. Weave this subplot into your main plot.

Where to Next?

It's time to close out the book, and for you to make a plan for what you're going to do next.

Outlining   Secrets   Unlocked

Chapter Seventeen: Where to Next After This Book?

After following the outlining sequence in this book, you have an outline that can turn your book dreams into a reality.

When you first have an idea for a book, you're meeting that idea as two strangers meet, and by writing this outline you're spending time with the idea and getting to know it.

You know an awful lot about your story idea now. In fact, you should take a moment to take stock of what that means. By following this process, you have started with a vague idea and made it live on its own.

This is a moment for celebration.

Get out the party hats, get out your happy music, and if cake is on your agenda, go and treat yourself.

Congratulations.

You are now a proactive outliner.

You understand that using a process unleashes your imagination, so you can spend time with your story, and not get bogged down with questions about what might happen next.

> **Your outline is one that will resonate with readers.**

You have added your artistry, your voice, your vision to make a unique story. And you have created your outline in a timely manner, banishing writer's block.

You have the momentum to take any of your scenes and get writing. This is a skeleton outline you can explore from one scene to another, but like a map, you now have the points the scenes must get to. This is powerfully exciting.

Writing a Novel Is an Amazing Accomplishment

We want to see you on bestseller lists, having readers write to you, telling you how your story touched their hearts. And that all comes from being in control of your writing.

With your outline, you can write smarter and faster. And if you use our book *Secrets to Editing Success: The Creative Story Editing Method*, you can use the process described there to edit and revise your story.

You have enough information to move from outlining to the next step.

The next step may involve research.

And here's the magic of our outlining process. You now know what to research.

The next step may involve outlining subplots.

And here's more magic of our outlining process. You now have a structurally sound plot to build your subplots around.

The next step may involve a deep dive into who your characters are, their backstory, or their motivations.

And here's more magic of our outlining process. You now know what characters need to be fleshed out.

If you love, love, love outlining, you may want to outline the rest of your scenes.

And here's more magic of our outlining process. You now have a process to do that.

The next step may be to start writing your draft.

And here's the final magic of our outlining process. You are starting that draft with a structurally sound outline.

You're the artist. You decide.

Benefits of Outlining a Novel

Let's look at what you have achieved.

You have an outline that is structurally sound.

And that knowledge is yours to harness whenever a new story idea hits. Wow. An outlining process for every story you want to write, and you can create story after story readers will love.

This will make writing your first draft easier. Why? Because you won't be second guessing yourself anymore. Yes, you can make any change to the outline, but what stands now is an underlying strong structure.

Writing a first draft is great. Getting that draft edited will be super satisfying, too. Why? Because you'll be starting the edit with a strong story structure, and you'll be confident the edits will turn into a strong revision plan.

Having an outlining process that is actionable and repeatable means you will gain confidence. You can guard against impostor syndrome, too.

Impostor syndrome can come from a knowledge vacuum. When you start with a strong plot outline, then you know you are starting your story from a strong place, and confidence is the best way to conquer impostor syndrome.

> **Telling stories is what makes us human. It opens our world, and we share our worldviews. As writers, we have a job to do, and we should do that job as best we can. Readers out there need the book you just outlined.**

Where to Next?

The choice is yours. You are the artist. From here you can:
- Start writing your draft.
- Outline at the scene level.
- Outline subplots.
- Rework your outline into a more complex structure.

> **Whatever you choose, we know you've got a great story outlined.**

Please tell us you're amazed at how easy it was to create a story outline. We'd love it if you posted a review for us.

We started this book by saying:

> **Everyone reading this book has a dream. You want to write a novel. Scratch that, you want to write a novel readers love.**

We know our outlining method has helped you get one step closer to that dream.

Glossary

Glossary

Act 1

The first quarter of the novel, where the characters, the main story goal and the stakes are all shown to the reader. This is Aristotle's beginning.

Act 2

From Plot Point 1 to Plot Point 2, and everything in between. This is Aristotle's middle.

Act 3

Everything after plot point 2 through to the climax and the resolution. This is Aristotle's end.

Action Scene

Movement and dialogue dominate the scene.

Action / Sequel

The two types of scenes in a book. One is the fast-paced high energy scene. The other is slower, where the character is reacting to an action scene.

Antagonist

The character who is in direct opposition to the protagonist and stands between the protagonist and the story goal.

Bestseller

A book readers love, we believe, mainly as it is structurally sound.

Blurb

Readers buy a book on its promise. This promise is the description of the story that includes who the protagonist is, what their main story goal is, and what's at stake if they don't achieve the main story goal.

Blurb Promise

The reason a reader buys the book. They want the book to be about what the blurb says. Successful books keep this promise.

Chapter

The portion of a novel made up of a single scene or multiple scenes.

Character

A person or animal or other being who is in a story.

Climax

The scene at the end of the story where the story goal is addressed. It is the scene with the biggest emotion and word count compared to those close by it.

Combined Protagonist

A combined protagonist is two main characters where both characters want the same thing, meaning their goal for the story is the same. In their struggle to achieve the goal, they will both suffer or benefit from the same events.

Conflict

Action that pits two or more characters against each other.

Draft (Manuscript or Novel)

An umbrella term that can cover any unpublished work in progress from the first draft through to the final draft.

External Goal

What a character wants in the story, not what they want in life.

Glossary

Fiction

Stories based on made-up events.

Fictionary

The company that created StoryTeller and StoryCoach.

Group Protagonist

The protagonist entity is a group of characters, a world, or a society.

Inciting Incident

The inciting incident contains the action that changes or disrupts the protagonist's ordinary life.

Main Character

The protagonist.

Main Event

The key action that takes place in a scene.

Manuscript

An unpublished book.

Middle Plot Point

The middle plot point scene should have something terrible or life-changing happen to the protagonist.

Non-Story Arc Scenes

Scenes in a manuscript that are not the inciting incident, plot point 1, the middle plot point, plot point 2, or the climax.

Pantser

A writer who doesn't outline their story before writing it. Often referred to as a discovery writer.

Plot

What happens in the story.

Plot Point 1

The moment in the story when the protagonist accepts the story goal.

Plot Point 2

The moment in the story when the protagonist is at their lowest emotional or physical state.

Point of View (POV)

The story or scene is filtered from one character's perspective. This filtering shows the reader what the character is like.

Point of View Character

The character who the reader will experience the scene through.

Protagonist

The main character in a story.

Protagonist Entity

A protagonist made up of one or more characters.

Resolution

This is everything after the climax scene and up to the last word.

Scene

A portion of a story where characters do something. A scene will have a beginning, a middle, and an end.

Scene Climax

A portion of the scene where the POV goal is addressed.

Scene Middle

A portion of the scene between the opening hook and the scene climax.

Scene Name

The description of a scene in three words or fewer.

Skeleton Blurb

    Story Level Skeleton Blurb:
    Shows the protagonist, their story goal, and what's at stake if they don't achieve their goal.

    Scene Level Skeleton Blurb:
    Shows the POV character, their POV goal, and what if goals fails for the scene level.

Skeleton Synopsis

Six paragraphs that tell the story, using the blurb in the first paragraph and the 5 story arc scenes filling the rest of the paragraphs. The ending must be revealed.

Story

A narrative that has an inciting incident, a plot point 1, a middle plot point, plot point 2, a climax, and a resolution.

Story Arc

A diagram showing the location of the inciting incident, plot point 1, middle plot point, plot point 2, and climax in a story.

Story Goal

What the protagonist must achieve in the story. A reason for the reader to read.

Story Stakes

These are the consequences for the protagonist if they do not achieve the story goal.

Synopsis

A short summary of the story that includes the protagonist, the story goal, and the main plot points and the story's ending.

Tension

The anticipation that something bad or good will happen.

What If Goal Fails

These are the consequences that will happen to the POV character if they do not succeed at the POV scene goal.

Index

A

Act 1 15, 19, 49, 53, 67, 69-73, 75, 83, 86, 90-91, 96-97, 100, 126, 128, 130, 144, 150, 153, 166, 233, 240, 249

Act 2 15, 19, 29, 49, 52-53, 69, 73, 90, 95-98, 100, 106, 110, 114-115, 128-131, 133, 138, 150-151, 153-154, 234, 249

Act 3 15, 19, 42, 49, 51, 53, 69, 110, 133-134, 137, 150, 152-153, 155, 234-235, 239-240, 249

Action Scene 51, 80-81, 96, 98, 117, 119, 136, 142, 239, 249

After-Draft Outline 158

Antagonist 59, 105, 144, 249

B

Bestseller 10, 13, 71, 244, 249

Blurb 14, 19, 22-23, 25-29, 32, 35-36, 38, 41-42, 44-47, 49-59, 61-64, 72, 74-75, 77, 79, 81-90, 92, 95, 97, 99-102, 105-106, 108-109, 117-120, 124-125, 127, 135, 137, 141, 143-144, 146, 149, 161, 163-171, 183-184, 186-190, 193-194, 197-198, 201, 205-215, 217, 220-222, 228-229, 233, 239, 241, 249-250, 253

C

Character Entrance and Exit
    Character Arc 16

D

Draft 9, 11, 16-17, 47, 50, 54, 66, 70-71, 76, 97, 110, 143, 149, 157-158, 161, 164, 171, 179, 181-182, 186, 188, 212, 215, 220, 222-223, 245-246, 250

F

Fictionary Story Arc Scenes
    Climax 15, 21, 42, 44, 49, 51-54, 58, 60, 63-66, 78, 82, 91, 93, 98, 112, 114, 116, 133-136, 139-147, 152, 155, 159, 161-164, 169, 172-173, 175-179, 181-182, 185, 187-188, 190-192, 194-195, 198-215, 219, 221, 226-227, 229-233, 235, 237, 239-240, 249-253

    Inciting Incident 15, 19, 42, 44-45, 49-52, 54, 56-63, 65-66, 71-74, 76-92, 98, 110, 112-113, 115, 122, 126, 128, 130, 138-139, 150, 153, 159, 161, 172, 174, 181-183, 188-196, 199, 201-202, 204-205, 208, 217-218, 226, 229-233, 235-237, 251, 253

    Middle Plot Point 15, 20, 42, 44, 49, 52-54, 57, 59-60, 62, 64-66, 70, 78, 82, 91-92, 95-103, 105-107, 109, 111-

121, 123–124, 129, 131, 151, 154, 159, 161, 172, 181–182, 210–213, 215, 218, 226, 229, 232, 234, 236–237, 251, 253
Plot Point 1 15, 20, 42–45, 49–52, 54–66, 71–73, 78, 82, 86–89, 91–92, 95–109, 111, 113, 115, 119, 128–131, 150–151, 153, 159, 161, 167–168, 170–172, 181–184, 186–187, 189, 192–193, 195–197, 199–201, 203–205, 218, 226, 229, 232, 234–236, 249, 251–253
Plot Point 2 15, 20–21, 42–44, 49–51, 53–54, 57–60, 62–66, 78, 82, 91, 93, 98, 100–103, 105, 112, 114–116, 122, 124–128, 130, 132–138, 150, 152, 155, 159, 161, 172, 181–182, 196–198, 200–201, 203–205, 207, 218–219, 226, 229–230, 232–235, 237, 249, 251–253

Fictionary Story Elements
  Backstory 69–70, 244
  Character Arc 16
  Character in Motion 173
  Conflict 33–34, 65, 69, 95, 97, 102, 140, 177, 250
  Entry Hook 162–163, 174–178, 182, 185, 187–188, 190–192, 194–195, 198–200, 202–204, 207, 209, 211–212, 214
  Exit Hook 162–164, 173, 176–178, 182, 185, 187–188, 190–192, 194–195, 198–204, 207, 209, 212, 214
  Flashback 225–231, 235–237
  Objects 177
  POV 162–163, 165–171, 173–177, 179, 182–184, 186–195, 197–204, 206–207, 209, 211, 214, 252–254
  POV Goal 162, 167–168, 170, 182, 184, 186–188, 190–195, 198–204, 207, 209, 211, 214, 253
  Revelation 177
  Scene Climax 162–163, 173, 175–179, 182, 185, 187–188, 190–192, 194–195, 198–204, 207, 209, 212, 214, 253
  Scene Middle 162–163, 176–177, 182, 185, 187–188, 190–192, 194–195, 198–200, 202–204, 207, 209–210, 212, 214, 253
  Scene Name 73, 162–163, 176, 179, 182, 185, 187–188, 190–192, 194–196, 199–204, 207, 209, 212, 214, 253
  Story Arc 15–16, 19, 22, 42–45, 48, 53–56, 59, 61, 66, 69, 74, 80, 87, 90–91, 96, 105, 141, 145, 161, 164, 168, 170–171, 179–182, 188, 196, 210, 212, 215, 217, 219–220, 225–233, 240, 251, 253

Tension 31, 33–34, 71–72, 75, 84, 86, 97, 102, 135–137, 140, 144, 166, 170, 173, 178, 183, 187, 254

G

Genre 11, 13, 31–32, 99, 161

Goals

Internal Goals 30

Story Goal 15–16, 20–21, 23–27, 29–38, 41, 43, 45, 49–55, 58, 63–64, 71–74, 77–79, 83–89, 91–92, 95–102, 105–106, 111, 113, 115, 117, 120–121, 123–125, 127–128, 130, 133, 136–142, 150, 152–153, 155, 159, 163, 165–166, 169, 183–185, 188–189, 197, 205, 207, 209, 218–219, 221–222, 227–229, 233–237, 239, 241, 249–250, 252–254

M

Main Character 36–37, 240, 250–252

P

Prologue 74, 76, 228

Protagonist, Types of

Combined Protagonist 37, 221–222, 250

Group Protagonist 37, 221–222, 251

Protagonist 14–16, 19–21, 23–38, 43, 45, 49–59, 61–64, 71–72, 74–77, 80–81, 83–84, 86–87, 95–97, 100–102, 105–106, 117, 119–120, 124–125, 133–140, 142, 145, 147, 152, 155, 159, 165–166, 168, 170, 182–183, 188–189, 196–197, 205, 210, 215, 217–223, 227, 229, 231–232, 234–235, 237, 239, 241, 249–254

Protagonist Entity 37, 221–223, 251–252

R

Resolution 15, 21–22, 42, 54, 60, 98, 116, 133–134, 142, 145–147, 152, 155, 159, 217, 219, 235, 237, 249, 252–253

Revise 66, 244–245

Revision Plan 245

S

Scene 12, 14–16, 19, 21–22, 24, 29, 42–45, 48–56, 58–61, 63, 65–66, 69–74, 76–77, 79–81, 83–92, 95–101, 103, 105–

107, 109, 115–120, 123–127, 133–147, 149, 161–215, 217, 219–223, 226–233, 235–237, 239–241, 244, 246, 249–254
Scene Name   73, 162–163, 176, 179, 182, 185, 187–188, 190–192, 194–196, 199–204, 207, 209, 212, 214, 253
Skeleton Synopsis   15, 19, 41–42, 44–45, 47–48, 53, 67, 147, 217, 241, 253
Story Elements   16, 161–165, 171–173, 182, 188–189, 197, 206
Story Stakes   23, 25–27, 29, 32–35, 38, 41, 74, 89, 165–166, 254
StoryTeller   15, 251
Act 1   15, 19, 49, 53, 67, 69–73, 75, 84, 86, 90–91, 96–97, 100, 126, 128, 130, 144, 151, 154, 166, 233, 240, 251

Act 2   15, 19, 29, 49, 52–53, 69, 73, 90, 95–98, 100, 106, 110, 114–115, 128–131, 133, 138, 151–152, 154–155, 234, 251

Act 3   15, 19, 42, 49, 51, 53, 64, 69, 110, 133–134, 137, 151, 153–154, 156, 234–235, 239–240, 251

Action Scene   51, 80–81, 96, 98, 117, 119, 136, 143, 239, 251

After-Draft Outline   158

Antagonist   59, 105, 144–145, 251

B

Bestseller   10, 13, 71, 244, 251

Blurb   14, 19, 22–23, 25–29, 32, 35–36, 38, 41–42, 44–47, 49–59, 61–63, 65, 72, 74–75, 77, 79, 81–90, 92, 95, 97, 99–102, 105, 107–109, 117–120, 124–125, 127–128, 135, 137, 141–147, 149, 161, 163–172, 183–184, 186–190, 193–194, 197–198, 202, 205–207, 209–213, 215–217, 220–223, 228, 230, 233, 239, 241, 251–252, 255

C

Character Entrance and Exit

Character Arc   16

D

Draft   9, 11, 16–17, 47, 50, 54, 66, 70–71, 75–76, 97, 110, 144, 150, 157–158, 161, 164, 171, 179, 181–182, 186, 188, 213,

215, 220, 223, 245–246, 252

F

Fictionary Story Arc Scenes

Climax 15, 21, 42, 44, 49, 51–54, 58, 60, 63–66, 78, 82, 91, 93, 98, 112, 114, 116, 133–135, 140–147, 153, 156, 159, 161–164, 169, 172–173, 175–179, 181–182, 185, 187–188, 191–192, 194–196, 199–213, 215, 219, 221, 226–227, 229–233, 235, 237–240, 251–255

Inciting Incident 15, 19, 42, 44–45, 49–52, 54, 56–62, 64–66, 71–74, 76–92, 98, 111, 113, 115, 122, 126, 128, 130, 138–139, 151, 154, 159, 161, 172, 174, 181–183, 188–196, 199, 201, 203, 205–206, 208, 217–218, 226, 229–237, 253, 255

Middle Plot Point 15, 20, 42, 44, 49, 52–54, 57, 59–60, 62, 64–66, 70, 78, 82, 91–92, 95–103, 105–110, 112, 114–121, 123–124, 129, 131, 152, 155, 159, 161, 172, 181–182, 210–216, 218, 226, 229, 232, 234, 236–237, 253, 255

Plot Point 1 15, 20, 42–45, 49–52, 54–66, 71–73, 78, 82, 86–89, 91–92, 95–102, 104–105, 107–111, 113, 115, 119, 129, 131, 151–152, 154, 159, 161, 167–168, 170, 172, 181–184, 186–187, 189, 192–193, 195–197, 200–201, 203, 205, 218, 226, 229, 232, 234–236, 251, 253–255

Plot Point 2 15, 20–21, 42–44, 49–51, 53–54, 57–60, 62–66, 78, 82, 91–92, 98, 100–103, 105–106, 112, 114–116, 122, 124–128, 130, 132–138, 151, 153, 156, 159, 161, 172, 181–182, 196–198, 201–202, 204–205, 208, 218–219, 226, 229–230, 232–235, 237, 251, 253–255

Fictionary Story Elements

Backstory 69–70, 245

Character Arc 16

Character in Motion 173

Conflict 33–34, 66, 69, 95, 97, 102, 140, 177, 252

Entry Hook 162–163, 174–178, 182, 185, 187–188, 191–192, 194–195, 199–204, 208–209, 212, 214

Exit Hook 162–164, 173, 176–178, 182, 185, 187–188, 191–192, 194–196, 199–204, 208, 210, 213, 215

Flashback 225–231, 236–237

Objects 177

POV 162–163, 166–171, 173–177, 179, 182–184, 186–195, 197–204, 206, 208–209, 212, 214, 254–256

POV Goal 162, 167, 169–171, 182, 184, 186–188, 190–192, 194–195, 198–204, 208–209, 212, 214, 255

Revelation 177

Scene Climax 162–163, 173, 175–179, 182, 185, 187–188, 191–192, 194–196, 199–204, 208–209, 212, 215, 255

Scene Middle 162–163, 176–177, 182, 185, 187–188, 191–192, 194–196, 199–204, 208–210, 212–213, 215, 255

Scene Name 73, 162–163, 176, 179, 182, 185, 187–188, 191–196, 199–205, 208, 210, 213, 215, 255

Story Arc 15–16, 19, 22, 42–46, 48, 53–56, 59, 61, 66, 69, 74, 81, 87, 90–91, 96, 106, 142, 146, 161, 164, 168, 170, 172, 179–182, 188, 197, 210, 213, 215, 217, 219–220, 225–233, 240, 253, 255

Tension 31, 33–34, 71–72, 75, 84, 86, 97, 102, 135, 137, 140, 144, 166, 171, 173, 178, 183, 187, 256

G

Genre 11, 13, 31–32, 99, 161

Goals

Internal Goals 30

Story Goal 15–16, 20–21, 23–27, 29–38, 41, 43, 45, 49–55, 58, 63–64, 71–74, 77–79, 83–89, 91–92, 95–102, 105–106, 111, 113, 115, 117, 120–121, 123–125, 127–128, 130, 133, 136–143, 151, 153–154, 156, 159, 163, 165–167, 169–170, 183–185, 188–189, 197, 206–207, 210, 218–219, 221–222, 227–230, 234–237, 239, 241, 251–252, 254–256

M

Main Character 36–37, 240, 252–254

P

Prologue 74, 76, 228

Protagonist, Types of

Combined Protagonist 37, 221-222, 252

Group Protagonist 37, 221-222, 253

Protagonist 14-16, 19-21, 23-38, 43, 45, 49-59, 61-64, 71-72, 74-77, 80-81, 83-84, 86-87, 95-97, 100-102, 105-106, 117, 119-120, 124-125, 133-140, 143, 145-146, 148, 153, 156, 159, 166, 168, 170-171, 182-183, 188-189, 197, 206, 211, 216-223, 227, 229, 231-232, 235, 237, 239, 241, 251-256

Protagonist Entity 37, 221-223, 253-254

R

Resolution 15, 21-22, 42, 54, 60, 98, 116, 133-134, 143, 145-147, 153, 156, 159, 217, 219, 235, 238, 251, 254-255

Revise 67, 244-245

Revision Plan 245

S

Scene 12, 14-16, 19, 21-22, 24, 29, 42-46, 48-56, 58-61, 63, 66-67, 69-74, 76-77, 79-81, 83-91, 95-101, 104, 106-110, 115-120, 123-127, 133-148, 150, 161-217, 219-221, 223, 226-233, 235-237, 239-241, 244-246, 251-256

Scene Name 73, 162-163, 176, 179, 182, 185, 187-188, 191-196, 199-205, 208, 210, 213, 215, 255

Skeleton Synopsis 15, 19, 41-42, 44-45, 47-48, 53, 67, 148, 217, 241, 255

Story Elements 16, 161-164, 166, 172-173, 182, 188-189, 198, 207

Story Stakes 23, 25-27, 29, 32-35, 38, 41, 74, 89, 165-166, 256

StoryTeller 15, 253

Acknowledgments

K. Stanley:

Thank you to L. Cooke for working with me on our second book. Your knowledge and enthusiasm amaze me every day.

Thank you to our Proofreading Editor, Sherry Leclerc.

Thank you to our four beta readers: Lisa Taylor, Heather Wood, Annette G., and Shane Millar. Thank you for correcting the errors. Any that are left all belong to us.

Thank you to our ARC readers. Those of you who went above and beyond amazed us with your insight. Brandi Bagdett, Debbie Frank, Hope Douglas, and Linda O'Donnell our book is better because of your talent and generosity.

Fictionary, the company, deserves a shout-out.

Mostly, thank you to my husband and lifelong partner in everything. Without him, none of this has meaning.

L. Cooke:

Thank you to K. Stanley for asking me to co-author another book with you. You make dreams come true.

Thank you to Sherry, Lisa, Heather, Annette, and Shane. You are amazing.

Thank you to the Fictionary Community. I look forward to talking about your stories with you every day.

Thank you to our ARC readers: Brandi Bagdett, Debbie Frank, Hope Douglas, and Linda O'Donnell.

Thank you to my writing, editing, and now outlining friends. A special shout out to all the Fictionary Certified StoryCoach Editors. I learn from you, continually.

Thank you to my parents, I am lucky to be your daughter.

Thank you to my children. I write for you. All the stories you are writing are brilliant beyond measure. And finally, to my husband, before you, I had always been told about love, read about it, seen it in others; you show me what love is, every single day.

About the Authors

K. Stanley

Combining her degree in computer mathematics with her success as a best-selling, award-winning author and fiction editor, K. Stanley founded Fictionary and is the CEO. Fictionary helps writers and editors create better stories faster with software, an online community, and training.

Her novels include The Stone Mountain Mystery Series and Look the Other Way. Her first novel, Descent, was nominated for the 2014 Arthur Ellis Unhanged Arthur for excellence in crime writing. Descent is also published in Germany by Luzifer-Verlag.

Blaze was shortlisted for the 2014 Crime Writers' Association Debut Dagger.

Her short stories are published in *The Ellery Queen Mystery Magazine*, and *Voices from the Valleys*. Her short story *When a Friendship Fails* won the Capital Crime Writer award.

Secrets to Editing Success: The Creative Story Editing Method, *The Author's Guide to Selling Books to Non-Bookstores*, and *Your Editing Journey* are her non-fiction books.

She is the Story Editing Advisor to The Alliance of Independent Authors and was on the board of directors for the Story Studio Writing Society.

L. Cooke

L. Cooke is a Fictionary Certified StoryCoach Editor and Business Development Manager at Fictionary. Lucy is the co-author of *Secrets to Editing Success: The Creative Story Editing Method.*

She is writing her first novel, *My Fairy Assassin*.

About The Authors

www.ingramcontent.com/pod-product-compliance
Lightning Source LLC
Chambersburg PA
CBHW031241504426
43191CB00006B/382